Your Key to Home

Your Key to Home

A Complete Guide from Dream to Doorstep and Beyond

JUSTIN McCURDY

www.justinskeytohomelife.com

For permission requests, contact:
Justin McCurdy
www.justinskeytohomelife.com

979-8-9948642-1-0 (Paperback ISBN)
979-8-9948642-0-3 (Hardcover ISBN)
979-8-9948642-2-7 (Ebook ISBN)

For my Mom.
She was the best.

We didn't have much money growing up, but we were rich in her love and in the people she taught us to be.

She never got her dream home. But she gave me everything that mattered.

Her dream lives on with every person I help achieve their dream of homeownership. I sincerely hope that my book will help you achieve yours.

CONTENTS

PREFACE

• • •

I ALMOST DIDN'T WRITE this book. For years, people told me I should—clients, colleagues, friends. And for years, I found reasons not to. Then one evening, a young couple sat at my kitchen table, overwhelmed and in tears, and I realized the problem wasn't that information didn't exist—it was that nobody was putting it together for regular families—the families that no one else wants to spend the time to help.

This book comes from nearly three decades of experience across every corner of the housing industry. Having worked in three different parts of the country, I've seen what works. But more than from professional experience, this book comes from growing up in poverty but never feeling poor, because my Mom filled our lives with love. She taught me that you don't need wealth to be wise with money.

My Mom is the reason I want to help people. She never got her dream home, but she gave me the values to help others achieve theirs. I wrote this for her, for that couple at my kitchen table, and for you.

With gratitude,

Justin

PART ONE
Preparing Your Foundation

CHAPTERS 1–8

THE FOUNDATION YOU BUILD TODAY DETERMINES THE HOME YOU CAN AFFORD TOMORROW.

CHAPTER 1

A Key to Something Greater

• • •

There are moments in childhood that stay with you forever. Sometimes they aren't loud or dramatic—they're quiet and soft—the kind of moments that settle into your memory because of how they shaped you, not because of how they looked.

For me, those moments came from watching my Mom try, again and again, to give us something she had always dreamed of but could never quite reach: a home of our own. She spent years trying to buy a newly built home—walking through model homes on weekends, visiting quick-move-in communities, sitting down with salespeople who'd run her numbers and then shake their heads. My Mom had fantastic credit. She worked incredibly hard to ensure that, even with limited financial means. But her income wasn't enough. Her debt-to-income ratio was always just out of range. It didn't matter how responsible she was with money—and she was—the math on paper never quite worked in her favor. There was always something standing between us and that front door.

I remember how quiet she would get on the drives home from those appointments. Not angry. Not even sad, exactly. Just deflated. Like something inside her had slowly let out its air. She would stare through the windshield, and I could tell her mind was somewhere else. Probably still in that model home. Probably imagining what it would feel like to cook in that kitchen. To sit on that porch. To finally have something that was ours.

My dad died when I was very young. I don't have many clear memories of him—just flashes, really. I remember riding with him on our riding lawn mower, heading out to feed our Holstein cow, T-bone. I remember fishing with him, just the two of us, not saying much but not needing to. I remember watching him play games with my sister at the dinner table, pretending to steal her food, while she squealed and laughed, and my Mom shook her head with a smile she couldn't hide. And then one day he was gone.

I woke up in the middle of the night for some reason. I don't know what pulled me out of sleep, but something did. I looked out the window and saw an ambulance sitting in front of our house with no lights on. Two people were loading a covered body into the back of the vehicle. I stood there for a moment, trying to understand what I was seeing. Then I slowly opened the bedroom door and saw my Mom sitting on the couch, sobbing with her head between her legs, trying so hard not to wake us up. I didn't go out to her. I went back and lay in bed, staring at the ceiling, trying to digest everything I had just seen. I was five years old.

A lot of people will tell you it's impossible to remember things that clearly when you're that young. And for a long time, I questioned my own memories. For decades, actually. I carried those images around with me and wondered if my mind had filled in the gaps or made things up. Then one day, I finally had the courage to ask my Mom about it. I told her exactly what I remembered—the ambulance with no lights, the covered body, her on the floor trying not to make a sound.

Her face went white as a ghost. She looked at me with the saddest eyes I've ever seen and told me my memories were exactly as the incident had happened. Then she apologized to me.

I said, "Why are you apologizing? You did nothing wrong."

I'm not sharing this for sympathy. I'm sharing it because of what it shows about my Mother. Her resilience. Her strength. What she did for my sister and me after that night was something special and unfathomable. Most people would have collapsed under that kind of weight—losing a husband, raising two small children alone, barely making ends meet. She stood strong. She kept going. And she still loved us exactly the way we needed and wanted to be loved. Her example gave my little sister and me the best things that reside in us today. And it was just the three of us, my Mom, my little sister, and me, against the world.

There's something about growing up without stability that never quite leaves you. Even now, decades later, I notice it. The way I check locks twice. The way I keep extra supplies on hand. The way I feel a deep, almost physical relief when I walk into a home that I know belongs to me. These habits come from somewhere. They come from those years of uncertainty, when home was always temporary and could be taken away if something went wrong.

POOR IN MONEY, RICH IN EVERYTHING ELSE

I want to be honest with you about something, because I think it matters for what I'm trying to share in this book. I grew up in poverty. We didn't have much. We were poor regarding money—there's no getting around that. But what I need you to understand is that we were never poor in the ways that really mattered. We were rich in my Mom's love. We were rich in the values she taught us. We were rich in the example she set every single day—what it looks like to work hard, stay positive, and keep going when things are difficult. We were rich in the people she was raising us to become.

My Mom was the best. I don't say that lightly, and I don't say it just because she was my Mother. I say it because I watched her, day after day, year after year, do things that most people would have said were impossible. She worked over eighty hours a week. *Eighty*. And still, amazingly, made time for my little sister and me. She made us feel like we were her entire world. On a limited income, she provided everything we needed. Everything. We had food on the table. We had clean clothes. We had school supplies. We had stability, structure, and routine. We had a home—maybe not one we owned, but a home nonetheless—because she made it one.

And we had her. Present. Attentive. Loving. Teaching us, even when we didn't realize we were being taught. I think about the choices she made, and they humble me. She could have given up. She could have let the weight of single parenthood and poverty crush her spirit. She could have become bitter, resentful, or defeated. But she didn't. She woke up every morning and chose to fight for us. She chose to believe that things could get better. She chose to model strength, grace, and perseverance, even when—especially when—things were hard.

That's the inheritance she left me. Not money. Not property. Something far more valuable—the knowledge of who I wanted to be and the belief that I could become that person through hard work and integrity.

THE LESSONS SHE TAUGHT ME

My Mom was a magician with money—she had to be. I used to watch her at the kitchen table, bills spread out in front of her, working through the math with pencil and paper. She knew exactly when each bill was due. She knew which ones had grace periods and which ones didn't. She knew how to stretch a grocery budget so far that I honestly don't know how she did it.

She wasn't just surviving. She was strategizing. She was planning. She was building something stable for us out of resources that would have defeated most people. And here's the thing—without realizing it at the time, I was learning. Every time I watched her work through those numbers, every time I heard her explain why we were waiting until next week to buy something, every time I saw her make a way out of no way—I was getting an education that no classroom could have given me.

She taught me that you don't need a lot of money to manage it well. She taught me that discipline and planning matter more than income. She taught me that even when resources are tight, you can still make smart decisions—you just have to be intentional about every single dollar.

She taught me how to build credit on a limited income. She taught me how to prioritize. She taught me how to say no to things I wanted, so I could say yes to things I needed. She taught me delayed gratification before I ever knew there was a term for it.

I remember asking her once why we couldn't just buy something I wanted. I was maybe ten years old, and there was a toy or a game that all my friends had. She sat me down and explained, in terms I could understand, that money is a tool. You can use it wisely or waste it, but once it's gone, it's gone. She told me that every dollar we spent on something we didn't need was a dollar we couldn't spend on something we did need—or save for something important in the future.

It was a simple lesson, but it stuck with me. It shaped how I think about money to this day. Everything I know about managing money—the foundation of everything I'm going to share with you in this book—started with her at that kitchen table, watching her work miracles with almost nothing.

WHY I WANT TO HELP

My Mom is the reason I do what I do. She's the reason I get up every day wanting to help families achieve homeownership, and why I'm willing to spend time with people that others in my industry might pass over.

She taught me what it feels like to dream about something that seems out of reach. She taught me what it feels like to be told no, again and again, by people who look at your numbers and shake their heads. And she taught me what it feels like to want something so badly for your family and to keep hitting walls.

But she also taught me that walls can come down. That "no" doesn't have to be forever—that with the right knowledge, the right planning, and someone willing to help, things can change.

I want to be that someone for you. The person who's willing to sit with you and explain things clearly. The person who doesn't judge where you're starting from. The person who believes you can get there, even if it takes time.

My Mom never got her dream home. She passed away from cancer at the age of fifty-three, still dreaming about that kitchen, that porch, that backyard. And for a long time, that broke my heart. I'd spent my whole career helping other families get what my own Mother never could.

But somewhere along the way, I started seeing it differently. Her dream didn't die with her. It lives on in every family I help. Every key I hand over carries a piece of what she wanted for us. Every time I watch a mom cry happy tears in her new kitchen, every time I see a family finally get their "yes" after years of "nos"—I feel like I'm honoring her memory in the most meaningful way I know how.

That's why I do this work. That's why I wrote this book. That's why I'm willing to spend time that others won't spend, explaining things that others won't explain, helping families that others might overlook—because everyone deserves a chance at homeownership. And everyone deserves someone in their corner who actually cares whether they succeed.

A MENTOR WHO SHOWED ME WHAT WAS POSSIBLE

When I was eight years old, my Mom signed me up for the Big Brother, Little Brother program. I think she knew I was struggling without a father. She watched me watch other kids get picked up by their dads, heard me stay quiet when friends talked about fishing trips, camping, and all the activities fathers and sons do together. She couldn't fill that space herself, no matter how hard she tried. So she found someone who could fill at least part of it.

My "big brother" was a land developer. I had no idea what that meant when I first met him. I just knew he seemed like the kind of person who understood how things worked. He was the first successful person I'd ever really known—the first person who showed me that the life I was living wasn't the only life possible.

He started taking me to construction sites on weekends. Not the finished neighborhoods with green lawns and families moving in—the raw ones. Fields of clay that were being carved into streets. Concrete foundations that were being poured. Wooden skeletons of houses rising against the sky. The places where homes were being birthed into existence.

I was fascinated. Completely hooked. While other kids my age were watching cartoons, I was watching excavators, framers, and plumbers, trying to understand how it all came together. I asked questions constantly—probably too many questions—but he never seemed annoyed. He answered everything, explained everything, and treated my curiosity like it mattered.

He introduced me to contractors, forepersons, and tradespeople. He showed me blueprints and explained how to read them. He talked about zoning, permits, and everything that has to happen before a single nail is driven. For a kid who'd grown up feeling like the world was full of closed doors, suddenly I was seeing how things actually got built.

But the lesson that stuck with me most wasn't about construction. It was about meaning. We were standing on a hill one Saturday afternoon, looking down at a cul-de-sac where six houses were going up. Workers swarmed over them. The air smelled like sawdust and fresh lumber.

"What do you see down there?" he asked me.

I shrugged. "Houses being built?"

He nodded slowly. "That's what most people see. But you know what I see? I see families. Kids who are going to grow up in those bedrooms. Parents who are going to cook dinner in those kitchens and watch their children play in those backyards. Couples who are going to sit on those porches and talk about their days." He put his hand on my shoulder. "We're not just building houses, Justin. We're building the places where people's lives happen. Every decision we make affects a family that's trusting us with their future. That's not something to take lightly."

Those words lodged themselves somewhere deep inside me, and they've guided everything I've done since. Every time I help a family buy a home, I remember standing on that hill. I remember that we're not just doing transactions. We're shaping the places where lives unfold, where children grow up, where memories are made. That's sacred work, even if the world doesn't always treat it that way.

BUILDING MY OWN FOUNDATION

I started working in construction when I was sixteen. Nothing glamorous—hauling lumber, sweeping up job sites, doing whatever grunt work needed doing. It was hard physical labor that left me exhausted at the end of every day. My hands got calloused. My back got strong. I learned what it meant to work.

For a kid who'd grown up in poverty, there was something powerful about building things. About creating something solid and permanent. About being part of giving families what my own family had never had.

Over the years, I worked my way through almost every part of the industry. I spent time on framing crews, learning how walls and roofs come together, how a structure becomes solid and true. I did landscaping, learning how the exterior of a home creates that crucial first impression. I worked in mortgage lending, learning the financial mechanics that make homeownership possible, understanding what lenders look for and why so many families get turned away.

Having worked in three different parts of the country, I've seen how regional differences affect the market—different customs, different price points, different challenges. But I've also seen what stays consistent everywhere with families: they want stability, a place to call their own, and someone they can trust to guide them through the process.

That mortgage work opened my eyes to something important. There were so many families out there just like mine. Families who desperately wanted homes, who were willing to work hard, but who didn't have the knowledge. They didn't understand how credit scores really worked. They didn't know what lenders were actually looking for. They had no idea that programs existed specifically designed to help people in their exact situations.

Some of these families had been told "no" so many times that they'd given up. They'd decided that homeownership was something that happened to other people. Luckier people. People who were somehow different from them.

But with the right guidance, many of them could actually qualify. The dream they'd given up on was still within reach. They just needed someone willing to spend the time to show them the way.

That's what I decided to become. Someone who'd take the time. Someone who'd help the families that everyone else overlooked. Just like my Mom would have wanted.

YOUR JOURNEY STARTS NOW

This book is organized into five parts, each building on the last:

1. Part One is about preparing your foundation—finances, credit, debt, budgeting, saving, and getting pre-approved.

2. Part Two walks you through the home-buying journey.

3. Part Three helps you turn your house into a home.

4. Part Four covers living your best home life.

5. Part Five looks at the bigger picture—building equity and legacy.

At the end, you'll find a glossary defining every term you need to know, plus resources including downloadable worksheets at www.justinskeytohomelife.com.

I don't know where you are as you read this. Maybe you're years away from buying. Maybe you're months away. Maybe you've been trying for a while, and you're starting to wonder if it will ever happen.

Wherever you are, I need you to know something: you can do this. I've seen families go from terrible credit to homeownership in two years. I've watched first-generation buyers achieve what their parents and grandparents never could. I've witnessed the transformation that happens when a family finally has a place to call their own—the pride, the stability, the sense of possibility that opens up.

That can be you. I truly believe that.

My Mom never stopped believing. Even when every door seemed closed, even when the numbers never added up, even when it would have been easier to give up—she held onto that dream. She kept walking through model homes. She kept imagining that kitchen, that porch, that backyard.

I'm asking you to do the same. Hold onto your dream. Believe that it's possible, even if you can't see exactly how you'll get there yet. Trust the process. Do the work. Take it one step at a time.

And let me help you get there.

Turn the page. Your journey home starts now.

CHAPTER 2
Understanding Your Financial Foundation

• • •

I NEED TO ASK you something, and I need you to be completely honest with me. Not the kind of honesty where you fudge the numbers a little to make yourself feel better. Not the kind where you round up your savings and round down your debt. I mean, really, uncomfortably honest.

What's your net worth?

If your mind just went blank, don't worry, you're not alone. I ask this question all the time—to families sitting across from me, excited and nervous about buying their first home—and about nine out of ten of them have no idea how to answer.

These aren't unintelligent people. They're college-educated, hard-working, responsible adults who pay their bills and have money in the bank. But they've never actually sat down and calculated the single most important number in personal finance—everything they own minus everything they owe.

I get why people avoid this. Numbers can be scary, especially when you suspect they might reveal something you don't want to see. It's easier to float along on a vague feeling that you're "probably okay" than to confront specific truths about your financial situation.

But here's the thing, you can't get where you want to go if you don't know where you're starting from.

Think about it this way. If someone called and asked for directions to your house, the first thing you'd ask is, "Where are you now?" Without a starting point, directions are useless. Just a bunch of lefts and rights that don't connect to anything real.

Your homeownership journey works the same way. That house you're dreaming about is the destination. But the path there begins wherever you are right now. And if you don't know exactly where that is—not vaguely, but specifically—you're just wandering and hoping for the best.

Hope isn't a strategy. Not for something this important.

CALCULATING YOUR NET WORTH

Net worth is simply what you own minus what you owe. No complicated formulas. No fancy software required. Just a clear-eyed accounting of where you actually stand.

Start by listing everything you own that has monetary value. Your checking and savings accounts—the actual balances, not what you wish they were. Retirement accounts like 401(k)s and individual retirement arrangements or accounts (IRAs). Investment accounts, if you have them. The current value of your vehicles—not what you paid for them, but what you could actually sell them for today—and any property you already own, and valuable personal items; though be conservative here.

Add all of that up. That's your total assets.

Now, list everything you owe. Every credit card balance, even the small ones you've been ignoring. Student loans—the full remaining balance. Car loans. Personal loans. Money you borrowed from family that you actually intend to pay back. Medical bills. Back taxes, if you have them. Anything and everything you owe to anyone.

Add all of that up. That's your total liabilities.

Subtract liabilities from assets. That number—whatever it is—is your net worth.

If it's positive, that's good. You own more than you owe. You have a foundation to build on, even if it's smaller than you'd like.

If it's negative—if you owe more than you own—don't panic. Millions of Americans, especially younger people carrying student loan debt, have negative net worth. It doesn't mean you're bad with money. It doesn't mean homeownership is impossible. It simply means you now know your starting point and can begin working on improving it.

The important part is knowing the truth. Because you can't fix what you can't see, and you can't build on a foundation you haven't measured.

I recommend calculating your net worth at least twice a year. Put it on your calendar. Make it a ritual. Watching that number change over time—hopefully growing, bit by bit—keeps you motivated when the daily grind of saving and sacrificing starts to feel pointless.

> •••RESOURCE•••
>
> If you want to make it easy on yourself, head over to www.justinskeytohomelife.com and check out the Free Home-buying Tools section. I built a free net worth calculator there, along with a bunch of other tools designed to help you through every step of this process.

THE DEBT-TO-INCOME RATIO

When you apply for a mortgage, the lender will calculate your debt-to-income ratio—DTI for short. This single number might be the most important factor in determining whether you're approved and what terms you qualify for.

DTI compares how much you pay toward debt each month to how much you earn. It tells lenders what percentage of your income is already spoken for before you even think about a mortgage payment.

There are actually two DTI ratios lenders consider. The front-end ratio compares just your proposed housing payment—principal, interest, taxes, insurance, and homeowner association (HOA) fees if applicable—to your gross monthly income. The back-end ratio compares all your monthly debt payments, including the proposed housing payment, to your gross income.

Most conventional loans require a back-end DTI of 43 percent or less. Some programs allow higher ratios, even up to 50 percent, with what are called "compensating factors"—like excellent credit, significant savings, or stable employment history that offset the higher debt load, though this varies by lender. Federal Housing Administration (FHA) loans sometimes approve borrowers with DTIs up to 50 percent in certain circumstances. In some cases, this can even go to 55–57 percent with strong compensating factors. Not all lenders will offer loans across all ranges, depending on their risk tolerances.

But here's something crucial you need to understand: Just because a lender approves a certain DTI doesn't mean you should take it.

Lending guidelines are designed to predict one thing—whether you'll default on your loan. They're based on statistical models of millions of borrowers that identify the maximum debt load most people can carry without missing payments.

What those guidelines don't predict is whether you'll be happy. Whether you'll have money left for date nights, vacations, and Christmas presents. Whether you'll be able to save for retirement or handle emergencies. Whether you'll actually enjoy living in the home you bought, or whether every single month will feel like a financial tightrope you're terrified of falling off.

I've watched families get approved for mortgages that were technically within guidelines, but left them stressed and stretched thin every month. "House poor," people call it—owning a nice home but unable to afford anything else. The house looks great from the outside, but inside, they're struggling.

That's not the dream you're working toward. That's a trap dressed up like success.

While you need to know what lenders will approve, more importantly, you need to know what actually works for your life. And those aren't always the same number.

TRACKING WHERE YOUR MONEY ACTUALLY GOES

Here's a notion that might sting a little. Most people have no idea where their money actually goes. They know the big stuff—rent, car payment, insurance, utilities. The predictable expenses that show up every month like clockwork. But everything else? The coffee runs, Amazon orders, subscription services, and quick trips to Target that somehow always cost $150? That money just vanishes. Twenty dollars here, fifty there. It never seems like much in the moment—until you add it up.

I've worked with families who discovered they were spending $500 a month on food delivery. Families were paying for gym memberships they had not used in years. Families with six different streaming services, when they really only watched one. Apps on their phones were charging monthly fees for features they'd long forgotten about.

I'm not saying any of this to make you feel bad. Life is busy. It's easy to lose track. We all do it to some degree. But every dollar that slips away unnoticed could move you closer to your goal. You can't plug leaks you don't know exist.

For the next sixty to ninety days, I want you to track every single dollar you spend. Every single one. Use an app if that works for you. Use a spreadsheet. Use a notebook and a pen. The method doesn't matter as long as you're consistent.

Capture everything. The mortgage or rent payment. The latte. The parking meter. The birthday gift you grabbed at the last minute. Everything.

At the end of that period, categorize everything. Housing. Transportation. Groceries. Dining out. Entertainment. Subscriptions. Personal care. Kids. Pets. Gifts. Miscellaneous. Be ruthlessly honest about what goes where. That daily coffee habit? That's dining out, not groceries.

This exercise will show you aspects of your spending that you literally can't see any other way. It might be uncomfortable. You might not like what you find. But it will also reveal exactly where you have room to redirect money toward what matters most.

WHAT MY MOM TAUGHT ME ABOUT BUDGETING

I learned budgeting from my Mom, and she didn't use any apps or spreadsheets. She used envelopes.

Every payday, she would cash her check and divide the money into different envelopes. One for rent. One for utilities. One for groceries. One for gas. And so on. Each envelope was labeled with what it was for and how much it needed to contain.

When she went to the store, she stuck to her budget. No impulse buys. No justifying extras. If the money she had set aside for groceries was spent, that was it for the pay period. No exceptions. No borrowing from other categories unless there was a genuine emergency. The system was simple, visual, and brutally honest.

If she wanted something that wasn't budgeted for, she had to find the money somewhere. Take it from another category and accept the consequence. Or wait until the next pay period. There was no pretending she had more than she did. The budget told the truth whether she wanted to hear it or not.

You don't have to use physical envelopes as she did—though some people still do, and it works great for them. But the principle applies to any budgeting system: know exactly what you have, decide in advance where every dollar needs to go, and then stick to the plan.

The key words there are "in advance." You decide before the money comes in. Before you're standing in a store. Before you're tempted. You make rational decisions when you're thinking clearly, not emotional decisions when you're tired or stressed or wanting to treat yourself.

Once you know your net worth, your DTI, and where your money currently goes, you can build a budget that actually supports your goal of homeownership.

SETTING A TIMELINE YOU CAN ACTUALLY HIT

One of the biggest mistakes I see is unrealistic timelines. Families who need two years of serious preparation, but are trying to buy in six months. Families who haven't addressed significant credit issues and are hoping to get approved next month. Families who have almost nothing saved and are expecting to close in ninety days.

It doesn't work. They either get denied outright or get approved on terms that aren't good for them: higher interest rates, bigger down payment requirements, and mortgage insurance. They could have avoided these if they'd just been patient.

Be honest with yourself about how much time you actually need.

Is your credit score below 620? Plan for at least twelve to eighteen months of focused credit building before you're likely to qualify for reasonable terms.

Do you have significant high-interest debt? Factor in time to pay it down until your DTI is comfortably within an acceptable range.

Is your down payment savings basically starting from zero? Calculate how long it will realistically take to accumulate your target amount at a sustainable monthly savings rate.

Add these up. Be honest. Don't fudge the numbers because you want to believe it will happen faster. A realistic timeline isn't a defeat—it's a strategy. It's the plan that actually gets you where you want to go, instead of the fantasy that keeps you spinning your wheels.

I've watched families who took eighteen months to properly prepare end up in dramatically better positions than families who rushed. The patient ones got better interest rates and lower monthly payments. They closed with emergency funds intact instead of drained. They started their homeownership journey on solid ground, not already stretched to the breaking point.

Patience isn't the enemy of your dream. Impatience is.

•••JUSTIN'S TIP•••

Don't be discouraged if your net worth is negative. Mine was too. What matters is knowing your starting point and making progress from there. I've watched families go from negative net worth to homeownership in two to three years by following a plan.

CHAPTER 3
Building Your Credit From the Ground Up

• • •

Let me tell you something I don't share with everyone. I've lost everything. Twice.

Twice in my life, I've watched my financial world crumble. I watched my credit score plummet to levels that made me wonder if I'd ever recover. I felt the shame and the fear and the overwhelming sense that maybe I'd never dig my way out.

The first time, I was younger—overextended, overconfident, unprepared for the curveballs life throws at you when you're not looking—and made mistakes that young people make. I thought I was invincible. I wasn't. The second time, I thought I knew better. I thought the lessons I'd learned would protect me. But circumstances I couldn't control combined with decisions I could have made differently, and there I was. Starting over. Again.

I'm telling you this because I want you to understand something important. I'm not writing this chapter from some ivory tower. I'm not someone who's always had perfect credit, looking down and lecturing you about what you should do. I've been in the pit. I've seen credit scores so low I was embarrassed to check them. I've been turned down, passed over, and told "no" by people who looked at my numbers and saw nothing but risk.

And I've rebuilt. Both times. Climbed from those depths all the way to the upper 800s. Proved to myself—and to anyone who bothered to look—that the past doesn't have to define the future.

If I can do it—twice—you can do it too.

WHY I'M PASSIONATE ABOUT HELPING

Here's what those experiences taught me. When you're struggling with credit, when your score is low, and when your options seem limited, almost nobody wants to help you.

Banks don't want to spend time with you; you're not profitable enough. Lenders see you as a risk, a liability, a problem to be avoided. Real estate agents would rather work with easy clients who already have everything in order—why waste time with someone who might not qualify? You become invisible—someone to be screened out, not served.

And that's exactly backwards.

The families who need the most guidance are the ones who get the least. The people who could benefit most from patient explanation, strategic planning, and genuine support are the ones everyone else gives up on or never bothers with in the first place.

That's why I do what I do. That's why I'll spend hours with families that other people in my industry wouldn't give ten minutes to. I remember what it feels like to be on the other side of that desk, hoping someone would just take the time to explain what I need to do. Hoping someone would see past the numbers to the person trying to do better.

My passion is helping people no one else wants to help. The families with imperfect credit. The buyers with complicated situations. The dreamers who've been told no so many times they've almost stopped believing yes is possible.

You deserve guidance. You deserve patience. You deserve someone who actually cares whether you succeed.

And honestly? I learned that from my Mom, too. She never made anyone feel bad for not having much. She helped when she could, with whatever she had. She treated everyone with dignity and respect, regardless of their circumstances. That's the example she set, and it's the one I try to follow every day.

WHAT YOUR CREDIT SCORE ACTUALLY MEASURES

Your credit score is a three-digit number that tells lenders how risky it is to lend you money. The higher the number, the less risky you appear. The less risky you appear, the better interest rates and terms you qualify for. And in mortgage terms, better rates can mean tens of thousands of dollars saved over the life of your loan.

Most credit scores range from 300 to 850. Different lenders have different thresholds, but here are some general guidelines.

For conventional mortgages, you typically need at least a 620 to qualify, though guidelines vary by lender (Source: Fannie Mae Selling Guide). FHA loans can go as low as 580, sometimes even 500, if you have a larger down payment (Source: HUD Handbook 400.1). But qualifying isn't the only goal—the higher your score, the better your terms. Those with scores above 740 typically get the best available rates.

Your score is calculated from five factors, and understanding them is the key to improving strategically rather than just hoping for better results.

Payment history is the biggest factor, accounting for about 35 percent of your score. This measures whether you pay your bills on time. Late payments hurt, especially recent ones. Collections, charge-offs, bankruptcies, and foreclosures hurt even more. The good news is that the impact of negative items diminishes over time.

Credit utilization is next, about 30 percent. This measures how much of your available credit you're currently using. If you have a credit card with a $10,000 limit and a $5,000 balance, your utilization on that card is 50 percent. That's too high. Lenders prefer utilization below 30 percent, and below 10 percent is even better.

Length of credit history accounts for about 15 percent. They look at how long you've had credit accounts open: the age of your oldest account, the age of your newest account, and the average age of all accounts. A longer history is generally better.

Credit mix is about 10 percent. Lenders like to see that you can responsibly manage different types of credit, such as credit cards, installment loans, and a mortgage. But don't open accounts just to diversify; this factor isn't worth the risk of new inquiries and potential missteps.

New credit is the final 10 percent. This looks at recent credit inquiries and newly opened accounts. Too many of these in a short period makes you look desperate for credit, which is a red flag.

GETTING YOUR CREDIT REPORTS

Before you can improve your credit, you need to know exactly what's on your reports. You're entitled to free reports from each of the three major bureaus—Equifax, Experian, and TransUnion—once per year through AnnualCreditReport.com. This is the official site. Don't get confused by lookalikes that want to charge you.

When you receive your reports, review them carefully. Verify that all the accounts listed are actually yours. Verify that the balances and payment histories are accurate. Look for any collections or negative items you don't recognize.

Errors are more common than you might think. If you find something wrong, dispute it with the bureau in writing. They're required to investigate and respond within thirty days. Getting errors removed can sometimes give your score an immediate boost.

Also, watch for signs of identity theft—accounts you never opened, addresses you've never lived at, inquiries from companies you've never contacted. If you see anything suspicious, act quickly to protect yourself.

REBUILDING AFTER A FALL

If you're rebuilding from a low point—like I did, twice—here's what actually works.

First, accept where you are. I know that's hard. I know the shame that comes with checking your credit score and seeing a number that feels like a grade on your worth as a person. But it's not. It's just a number—a snapshot of past financial behavior. And numbers can change.

Payment history is the biggest factor, so protecting it as you move forward is crucial. Set up automatic payments for at least the minimum on every single account. One late payment can undo months of careful progress. Make on-time payments absolutely non-negotiable, even if you're only paying minimums.

Here's what I personally do, and it has never let me down. I use the calendar on my phone to set a monthly reminder for each bill, scheduling it at least five days before the actual due date. That buffer gives me time to deal with anything unexpected—a bank delay, a weekend, whatever—without ever risking a late payment. I also check the billing cycle date for each of my credit cards so I know exactly when interest is calculated and my balance is reported. I make sure I pay the balance in full before that date, which keeps my reported balance low and avoids unnecessary interest charges. It takes a little time to set up, but once it's in place, it runs like clockwork.

Reducing credit utilization often produces the fastest visible improvements. Pay down credit card balances to get your utilization under 30 percent. Under 10 percent is even better. If you can't pay down balances immediately, consider asking for credit limit increases—same balance with a higher limit equals lower utilization percentage.

Don't close old credit cards, even if you're not using them. Closing accounts shortens your average credit history and reduces your total available credit, both of which can hurt your score.

Instead, use old cards occasionally for small purchases and pay them off immediately.

Avoid opening new accounts unless absolutely necessary. Each application creates a hard inquiry, which can temporarily ding your score. Remember, new accounts lower your average credit age.

If you have very thin credit or are rebuilding from scratch, consider a secured credit card. You put down a deposit that becomes your credit limit, and use it responsibly. After several months of good behavior, many secured cards are converted to regular cards, and your deposit is returned.

Be patient. This is the hardest part, but it's essential. Negative items fade over time. Most stay on your report for seven years, but their impact on your score diminishes well before they disappear. What hurt you three years ago matters less than what you're doing today.

When I was rebuilding, I didn't see dramatic changes overnight. There were months of discipline, of careful attention, of watching the number inch upward point by point. It felt slow. Sometimes it felt hopeless. But it wasn't. Step by step, month by month, the score climbed. It will for you too. I promise.

YOU'RE NOT YOUR CREDIT SCORE

Before we move on, I want to say something that I wish someone had said to me during my lowest financial moments. Your credit score didn't define your worth as a human being. It's a number. A useful number for certain purposes, but just a number. It doesn't measure your character. It doesn't measure your value as a parent, spouse, friend, or person. It doesn't measure your intelligence, kindness, work ethic, or potential.

Bad things happen to good people. Unexpected job losses. Medical emergencies that drain savings and max out credit cards. Divorces that destroy carefully built financial plans. Economic downturns that hit you when you're most vulnerable. Sometimes credit takes a hit not because of irresponsibility, but because life happened and you did the best you could with impossible circumstances.

Whatever got you to where you are today, the path forward is the same: understand the system, make a plan, and execute it consistently over time. That's it. No magic, no shortcuts, no secrets they don't want you to know. Just steady, persistent progress, one payment at a time, one point at a time, one day at a time.

I've been where you might be right now. I've felt the weight of that number. And I'm here to tell you it can get better. It will get better. If you do the work, if you stay consistent, if you don't give up—it will get better. Let's keep moving forward. Together.

• • • KEY TAKEAWAY • • •

Keep your credit utilization below 30 percent on each card and overall. If you have a $1,000 credit limit, keep your balance below $300. Below 10 percent is even better for maximizing your score.

SCORE RANGE	RATING	MORTGAGE IMPACT
800–850	EXCEPTIONAL	BEST RATES AVAILABLE
740–799	VERY GOOD	EXCELLENT RATES, EASY APPROVAL
670–739	GOOD	SOLID RATES, STANDARD APPROVAL
580–669	FAIR	HIGHER RATES, MAY NEED FHA
300–579	POOR	DIFFICULT APPROVAL, HIGHEST RATES

Table 1: *Credit Score Ranges and Their Impact on Mortgage Approval*

• • • WATCH OUT • • •

Don't cancel old credit cards. Even if you don't use them, old accounts help your credit history length and available credit. Closing them can actually hurt your score. Cut up the card if you need to—just keep the account open. Many credit cards require them to be used occasionally, so buy a pack of gum or a drink every month and pay it off immediately to keep it open.

CHAPTER 4

BREAKING FREE FROM DEBT

• • •

LET'S TALK ABOUT SOMETHING nobody likes to talk about: debt. I know it's uncomfortable. I know it might even be painful, depending on your situation. Some of you might be tempted to skip this chapter entirely—to tell yourself it doesn't apply to you, or that you'll deal with it later, or that it's not that bad. I understand the impulse. I really do.

But we have to address this head-on, because the truth is that debt is one of the biggest obstacles standing between families and homeownership. It's not just about the monthly payments, though those matter. Debt affects your debt-to-income ratio (DTI), which determines how much house you can qualify for. It affects your credit score, which determines what interest rate you'll pay. It affects your ability to save for a down payment. And it also affects your stress levels, relationships, sleep, and quality of life.

I've met with families with good incomes and steady jobs, but they couldn't qualify for a mortgage because their debt load was too heavy. I've watched dreams get delayed—sometimes for years—because credit card balances, car payments, and student loans ate up too much of the budget.

But I've also watched families dig themselves out. Families who thought they were buried, who figured they'd be paying off debt forever, who had given up on ever owning a home. With the right strategy and enough determination, they paid it off. They got free. And then they bought their houses. If they can do it, you can too. Let me show you how.

UNDERSTANDING YOUR DEBT PICTURE

Before you can attack debt effectively, you need to know exactly what you're dealing with. Not a vague sense of what you owe. Specific numbers.

Make a list of every single debt you have. Every credit card, even the one with the small balance you keep forgetting about. Every loan—car, student, personal, whatever. Every medical bill. Everything.

For each debt, write down the current balance, the interest rate, the minimum payment, and the due date. This might feel overwhelming. Do it anyway. You can't fight an enemy you can't see.

Now add up all the minimum payments. This is your baseline—the amount you must pay each month just to stay in good standing. Compare this to your income. What percentage is already committed to debt before you even think about housing, food, or anything else?

If that percentage makes you uncomfortable, good. Use that discomfort as motivation. Channel it into action.

THE MOMENTUM METHOD

There are two main approaches to paying off debt, and the one that works best for you depends partly on math and partly on psychology.

The mathematically optimal approach is to focus on the debt with the highest interest rate first. You pay the minimum on everything else and throw every extra dollar you can find at that highest-rate balance. Once it's paid off, you take that payment amount and add it to what you're paying on the next highest-rate debt. Repeat until you're debt-free.

This approach minimizes the total interest you pay over time. If you follow it perfectly, you'll get out of debt faster and more cheaply than with any other method. On paper, it's the clear winner.

But the problem is that humans aren't math problems. And for a lot of people, this approach is really hard to stick with. If your highest-rate debt is also your largest balance—which is often the case—it can take months or even years before you see meaningful progress. That's demoralizing. It feels like running on a treadmill. And when progress feels invisible, people give up.

The alternative is what I call the "Momentum Method." Some people know it as the "debt snowball." Instead of ranking your debts by interest rate, you rank them by balance, from smallest to largest. You pay minimums on everything, then attack the smallest balance with every extra dollar. Once that's gone—and it will be gone soon, because it's the smallest—you take its payment and roll it into the next smallest balance. And so on.

Yes, you might pay a little more in total interest with this approach. But you get wins faster. You see the debts actually disappear. You build momentum—psychological momentum that keeps you motivated when the process feels endless.

I've watched the Momentum Method work for families who had tried other approaches and failed. There's something powerful about crossing a debt off your list, about seeing the number of accounts you owe actually shrink. It proves that progress is possible. It shows you can do this. And that belief often makes the difference between people who finish and people who quit.

HOW I DID IT

I want to tell you exactly what I did to lower my own debt so I could buy my first house, because I think it's important for you to know that everything I'm asking you to do in this chapter is something I've done myself.

At the time, I was on a fixed income. There was no raise coming. No bonus around the corner. No windfall on the horizon. I had what I had, and I needed to make it work. So I started looking at my monthly obligations and asked myself a hard question. *What am I willing to give up now to have something better later?*

The first thing I looked at was my car. I had a nicer vehicle at the time, one that I liked driving and made me feel good. But the monthly payment was eating into my budget, and I couldn't ignore it anymore. So I made a decision that a lot of people wouldn't make—I sold it.

Now, here's the part that matters. I didn't trade it in while I still had a payment on it. A lot of people do that, and the remaining balance on the old loan is rolled into the new loan. You end up owing more on the new car than it's worth before you even drive it off the lot. That's called "negative equity," and it's a trap. I wasn't about to dig myself out of one hole by digging another one right next to it.

Instead, I sold the car outright, paid off what I owed, and bought a cheaper, more reliable car that got me from point A to point B. It wasn't flashy. It wasn't what I wanted to be driving. But it was what I needed to be driving. I knew I'd be in that car for a couple of years, and I was at peace with that because I could see the bigger picture.

The monthly savings from the payment difference were significant. But what really made it work is that I kept paying myself the same amount I'd been paying on the old car. My new payment was lower, but I didn't pocket the difference. I took that extra money and used it to start my Momentum Method—rolling it into my smallest debt, then the next, and the next. That surplus became the engine that drove everything forward.

On top of that, I cut out every extra I didn't truly need. Subscriptions, dining out, impulse purchases—anything that wasn't essential went away. I got honest with myself about the difference between what I wanted and what I needed, and for that season of my life, needs won every time.

The thing that kept me going was a simple realization: a car is a depreciating asset. The moment you drive it off the lot, it's worth less than what you paid. Each month that passes, it loses more value. But a house? A house is an appreciating asset. It builds equity. It builds wealth. It gives your family a foundation that a car never will. I was willing to drive a humble car for a couple of years if it meant my future family would have a home.

I did all of this while I was single, and that was intentional. I knew that when I eventually met my wife, I didn't want to burden her with my financial struggles. I wanted to come into that relationship with my house in order, literally and figuratively. I wanted her to see someone who had done the hard work, made the sacrifices, and built something solid.

I saw it as short-term pain for long-term gain. And it worked. It worked very well.

I'm not sharing this to brag. I'm sharing it because I want you to see that these strategies aren't just theories in a book. They're real. I lived them. The Momentum Method, the sacrifice, the discipline—it all added up to a mortgage approval and a set of house keys in my hand. If it worked for me on a fixed income without shortcuts, it can work for you, too.

FINDING EXTRA MONEY TO THROW AT DEBT

The spending tracking exercise I asked you to do earlier? This is where it pays off.

Look at your categorized expenses and start asking hard questions. What subscriptions are you paying for that you don't really use or could live without? What dining-out costs can be reduced without making you miserable? What shopping is impulse rather than necessity?

I'm not saying you have to live like a monk. Life should have some enjoyment. If cutting absolutely everything leaves you depressed and resentful, you won't stick with it anyway. But if you're serious about getting out of debt and buying a home, temporary sacrifice is part of the deal.

Look at your recurring bills, too. Can you negotiate a lower car insurance rate? Shop around for better internet options and phone service? Raise deductibles to lower premiums if you have adequate emergency savings? These aren't exciting victories, but they add up.

And consider whether you can bring in extra money, even temporarily: selling things you no longer need or use, picking up occasional freelance or gig work in your spare time, and asking for overtime if it's available at your job. Every extra dollar you can direct toward debt repayment is a dollar that accelerates your progress.

DEALING WITH HIGH-INTEREST DEBT

If you have credit card debt at 20 percent or higher interest, that should probably be your top priority, regardless of which method you choose. Interest that high compounds brutally. A $5,000 balance at 24 percent interest grows by $100 per month in interest alone. You're running uphill against a treadmill going the wrong direction.

Consider balance transfer options if you have good enough credit. Some cards offer zero percent intro rates for twelve to eighteen months, letting you make real progress without interest piling on. But be careful: read the terms carefully, have a plan to pay it off before the promotional period ends, and don't run up new balances on the original cards.

Personal loans can sometimes consolidate high-rate credit card debt into a single payment at a lower rate. But, again, only if you won't just re-accumulate credit card debt once the cards are paid off. Consolidation only works if it's paired with changed behavior.

THE DEBT YOU SHOULD KEEP

Not all debt is equally problematic. Low-interest debt that's being paid down steadily doesn't need to be your top priority.

A car loan at 4 percent? Make your payments, but don't stress about paying extra. That money probably does more good going toward high-interest debt or savings.

Student loans, depending on your rate and situation, may also fall into this category. If you're on income-driven repayment and working toward forgiveness, the calculation is different from if you're just paying them down normally.

The goal is strategic allocation of limited resources. Not all debt is the same, and treating it all the same wastes money you could be using better elsewhere.

PROTECTING YOUR PROGRESS

Getting out of debt isn't a sprint; it's a marathon. It takes time—months at minimum, often years—depending on how much you owe. You need strategies to stay motivated and avoid backsliding.

First, build a small emergency fund even while you're paying off debt. I know this seems counterintuitive. Every dollar going to savings is a dollar not going to debt, right? But without at least a small cushion—$500 to $1,000 minimum—every unexpected expense becomes new debt. Your car breaks down, and suddenly you're adding to credit card balances instead of paying them down. The emergency fund protects your progress.

Second, track your payoff visually. Create a chart. Use an app. Put something on your wall that shows how far you've come. When you're grinding through month after month, that visual evidence of progress keeps you going.

Third, celebrate milestones appropriately. When you pay off a debt, acknowledge it. Not by going out and spending a bunch of money—that defeats the purpose—but by recognizing that you did something hard and you succeeded. Share the victory with someone who supports your goals.

Fourth, find accountability. Tell someone what you're doing. A spouse, a parent, a trusted friend. Someone who'll ask you about your progress and encourage you when you're struggling. Reporting to another person keeps you honest.

The path out of debt isn't glamorous. It's often boring and sometimes painful. But freedom is on the other side. And freedom is where your dream home lives.

CHAPTER 5

Saving for Your Down Payment

• • •

The down payment, for a lot of families, is the mountain that seems impossible to climb, especially if you're starting from zero or close to it. And I get it. We're talking about thousands of dollars—sometimes tens of thousands—that you need to accumulate somehow while also paying rent and bills and trying to live your life. When you look at that number all at once, it can feel overwhelming. Impossible, even.

But what I've learned after helping hundreds of families through this process is that the down payment obstacle is usually more manageable than people think—sometimes much more so.

The families who succeed aren't necessarily the ones with the highest incomes. They're the ones who understand their real options, make strategic choices, and stay consistent over time. That's it. No special advantages. No windfalls required. Just knowledge, planning, and persistence. Let me show you what they know.

HOW MUCH DO YOU ACTUALLY NEED?

The traditional advice says you need 20 percent down to buy a home. For a $300,000 house, that's $60,000. For a $400,000 house, it's $80,000. No wonder people feel like homeownership is out of reach. Those are enormous numbers to save.

But the truth that the traditional advice often leaves out is that that 20 percent number isn't a requirement—it's one option among many—and for many families, it's not even the best option.

Conventional loans backed by Fannie Mae and Freddie Mac offer down payment programs as low as 3 percent for qualified first-time buyers. On that same $300,000 house, 3 percent is $9,000. Still significant, but a lot more achievable than $60,000.

FHA loans require just 3.5 percent down—$10,500 on our $300,000 example. And qualification requirements are more flexible than for conventional loans.

Veterans Affairs (VA) loans for eligible veterans and service members require no down payment. If you've served, this is one of the most valuable benefits you've earned. US Department of Agriculture (USDA) loans for rural and qualifying suburban areas also offer zero down for income-eligible buyers.

ZERO PERCENT DOWN CONVENTIONAL LOANS

There's something most people don't know about, and honestly, a lot of people in the industry don't talk about it enough. Some banks offer zero-percent down conventional portfolio loans. These are loans the bank keeps on its own books instead of selling to Fannie Mae or Freddie Mac, which means it can set its own rules.

What makes these programs remarkable is the combination of benefits. We're talking zero down payment, no private mortgage insurance (PMI), and in many cases a lower-than-market interest rate. Some of these programs don't even have an income cap, which means you don't have to fall under a certain income threshold to qualify. That's a big deal because a lot of assistance programs exclude families who earn a decent living but still struggle to save for a large down payment.

These portfolio loans are typically offered by community banks and credit unions that want to attract homebuyers to their institutions. The bank benefits by building a long-term customer relationship, and you benefit by getting into a home with significantly less cash upfront and better terms than you might find elsewhere.

The catch? You have to know they exist and ask. These programs aren't always widely advertised. They might not show up when you're shopping rates online. You often need to walk into a local bank or credit union and speak with a loan officer to find out what's available. This is one of those situations where doing your homework and asking the right questions can save you tens of thousands of dollars.

I always tell home buyers I work with to shop beyond the big national lenders. Talk to community banks. Talk to credit unions. Ask specifically about portfolio loan products with zero down and no PMI. You might be surprised at what's out there.

Now, there are trade-offs to putting down less regardless of which program you use. A smaller down payment results in a larger loan, which in turn leads to higher monthly payments. And having less equity from day one means less cushion if home values drop.

But for many families, the math still works. Paying a slightly higher monthly payment beats waiting a decade or more to save 20 percent—especially when you factor in rising home prices and rents in the meantime. By the time you've saved 20 percent, the house you were looking at might cost significantly more.

Run the numbers for your specific situation. Don't assume 20 percent is the only path.

DOWN PAYMENT ASSISTANCE PROGRAMS

Here's something that surprises most people. There are literally thousands of programs out there specifically designed to help with down payments and closing costs. Grants that don't need to be repaid. Forgivable loans that disappear after you live in the home for a certain period. Low-interest loans with favorable terms.

These programs are offered by state housing finance agencies, cities, counties, nonprofit organizations, and even some employers. Most are targeted at first-time buyers, but the definition of a "first-time buyer" is often broader than you'd expect—many programs count you as a first timer if you haven't owned a home in the past three years.

Income limits usually apply—these programs are designed for moderate-income families, not high earners. But "moderate income" often extends higher than people expect, especially in higher-cost areas. There are purchase price limits, too, and most require that you live in the home as your primary residence. Some also require completing a homebuyer education course.

To find programs you might qualify for, start with your state housing finance agency. Every state has one. They maintain comprehensive lists of available assistance in your area. The US

Department of Housing and Urban Development also lists approved housing counseling agencies that can help you identify options.

Don't assume you don't qualify. Check. You might be surprised.

And don't think of this as charity. These programs exist because stable homeownership benefits communities. Cities and counties want residents who are invested in their neighborhoods. Employers want workers who aren't constantly on the move. Everyone benefits when families achieve stable housing.

BORROWING FROM YOUR RETIREMENT ACCOUNT

If you have a 401(k) or similar retirement account through your employer, you may have another option for funding your down payment that a lot of people overlook: borrowing from yourself.

Most 401(k) plans allow you to take a loan against your balance. You're not withdrawing the money permanently—you're borrowing it from your own account and paying it back over time, with interest, and that interest goes back into your own account. It's essentially paying yourself back instead of paying a bank.

The typical limit is 50 percent of your vested balance or $50,000, whichever is less. Repayment terms are usually up to five years for a general-purpose loan, but many plans extend that to fifteen years or longer when the loan is used to purchase a primary residence. Payments are typically deducted directly from your paycheck, so there's no risk of forgetting or falling behind.

The advantages are real. There's no credit check, because you're borrowing your own money. The interest rate is usually lower than what you'd pay on a personal loan or credit card. And the interest you pay goes back into your retirement account rather than into a lender's pocket.

But there are risks you need to understand. While that money is out of your retirement account, it's not growing. You're missing out on potential investment returns during the repayment period. And if you leave your job—voluntarily or not—most plans require you to repay the full loan balance within a short window, often sixty to ninety days. If you can't, the outstanding balance is treated as a distribution, which means you'll owe income taxes on it and a 10 percent early withdrawal penalty if you're under fifty-nine and a half.

So this isn't a decision to make lightly. But for some families, especially those with a solid retirement balance and stable employment, it can be a smart way to access down payment funds without taking on additional debt or draining a savings account. Talk to your plan administrator and a financial advisor before making this move, and make sure you understand all the terms and risks.

GIFT FUNDS AND FAMILY HELP

If you have family members willing and able to help with your down payment, that can be a legitimate option. Most loan programs allow gift funds for all or part of your down payment.

But there are rules. The money needs to be truly a gift, not a loan you're expected to repay. You'll need a gift letter stating that no repayment is expected. And the lender will want to document the source of the funds and verify that it's not just a disguised loan that would affect your DTI.

Don't try to work around these requirements. Lenders are experienced at detecting undisclosed loans and other shenanigans. Getting caught can tank your loan approval and potentially constitute fraud.

If family help is available to you, there's no shame in accepting it. Families have been helping each other build wealth for generations. It's part of how economic mobility works. Just make sure it's done properly so it doesn't affect your loan approval.

STRATEGIC SAVING

Whether you're saving the whole down payment yourself or supplementing with assistance programs or family help, building that fund requires strategic effort.

Automate your savings. Set up automatic transfers from your checking account to a dedicated down payment account on the same day your paycheck hits. Treat this transfer exactly like a bill that must be paid. If the money moves before you see it in checking, you're far less likely to spend it on something else.

Keep your down payment savings completely separate. Use a different account—ideally at a different bank—than your regular checking. This creates friction. It makes it harder to access money on a casual basis. It removes the temptation to "borrow" from your down payment for other things. That friction is your friend.

Consider a high-yield savings account. Interest rates on savings accounts have improved significantly in recent years. Some online banks offer savings account rates above 4 percent. That's free money just for keeping your down payment in a smart place. Not a fortune, but every dollar helps.

Direct windfalls straight to the goal. Tax refunds. Work bonuses. Birthday money. Proceeds from selling stuff you don't need. Whenever unexpected money comes in, channel it immediately into your down payment fund. Don't let it sit in checking where it will gradually disappear into everyday spending.

Set intermediate milestones. If your ultimate goal is $15,000, celebrate when you hit $3,000, then $6,000, then $10,000. These smaller victories keep you motivated during what can feel like a very long slog. The goal seems less impossible when you've already proven you can make progress.

DON'T FORGET CLOSING COSTS

Your down payment isn't the only cash you'll need to bring to the closing table. There's also a substantial bill for closing costs—fees and expenses that typically run 2 to 5 percent of your loan amount.

On a $300,000 loan, that means $6,000 to $15,000 in closing costs on top of your down payment. If you're planning for a $9,000 down payment but haven't budgeted for closing costs, you're going to come up short.

Some of these costs can be negotiated or shopped for better deals. Some can be rolled into your loan in certain situations. And in some markets, you might be able to negotiate seller contributions toward closing costs as part of your purchase offer. But you need to have a realistic expectation of the total cash required.

Plan for both. Save for both. Don't let closing costs surprise you right when you're trying to close on your dream home.

Now, here's something worth knowing if you're considering new construction. Many builders across the country will pay all of your closing costs as long as you use their preferred lender and title company. All costs. That can save you thousands of dollars right off the top.

Some of the larger national builders own their own lending and title companies. That's how they can afford to cover closing costs—they're making money on the loan side, meaning they can absorb those costs on the sales side. It's a different business model that works for many buyers.

I've mostly chosen to work for local builders throughout my career, and there's a reason for that. Local builders tend to offer the same closing-cost benefit and many other perks that larger builders won't. But there's one key difference. Most local builders don't own the lender or title company they partner with. That means they aren't making any money off your loan. They have no financial incentive on that side of the transaction. The reason they want you to use their lender partner is simple—they trust them. If their lender says you can close, the builder knows the deal is solid. They don't have to worry about a finished house sitting on the market longer than planned.

And that matters more than people realize. Every month, a finished house sits unsold, it costs the builder real money in carrying costs—loan interest, insurance, taxes, maintenance. That financial pressure means builders are motivated to work with lenders who get deals closed on time, which usually translates into a smoother, better loan experience for you as the buyer. It's one of those situations where everyone's interests are aligned, and that's always a good place to be.

HOW LONG WILL THIS TAKE?

How long it takes to save your down payment depends on your target amount, your income, and how much you can realistically set aside each month.

Do the math. If you need $15,000 and save $500 per month, that's thirty months, or two and a half years. If you can push it to $750, that's twenty months. If you receive a $3,000 tax refund and direct it to savings, you further shorten the timeline.

The numbers don't lie, but they also don't have to be depressing. Every month of saving brings you closer to your goal. And the discipline you develop while saving will serve you well as a homeowner.

Some families can accelerate this process dramatically by making temporary lifestyle changes for a focused sprint: taking on a roommate, driving an older car longer, or cutting expenses ruthlessly. Others prefer a steadier approach that feels more sustainable in the long term. Neither is wrong—what matters is that you're making consistent progress.

The families who succeed are the ones who start. The ones who run the numbers, make a plan, and begin saving today instead of waiting for the perfect moment.

There's no perfect moment. There's just today. Start today.

HOME PRICE	3% DOWN	5% DOWN	10% DOWN	20% DOWN
$200,000	$6,000	$10,000	$20,000	$40,000
$250,000	$7,500	$12,500	$25,000	$50,000
$300,000	$9,000	$15,000	$30,000	$60,000
$350,000	$10,500	$17,500	$35,000	$70,000
$400,000	$12,000	$20,000	$40,000	$80,000

Table 2: Down Payment Amounts by Home Price and Percentage

•••WATCH OUT•••

Don't drain your savings completely for the down payment. You'll need reserves for closing costs, moving expenses, and an emergency fund. Lenders also want to see that you have money left after closing—usually two to three months of mortgage payments.

CHAPTER 6

UNDERSTANDING YOUR TRUE BUDGET

LET ME TELL YOU about a mistake I've seen families make over and over again.

First, they go to a lender. They provide their documentation, answer the questions, and get their credit pulled. And they get pre-approved for a certain amount—let's say $350,000. Then they start house hunting. And because the lender said $350,000, they shop for houses priced at $350,000. They stretch to the maximum, as if that preapproval number was a target to hit rather than a ceiling to stay under.

Six months later, they're in their new house. And they're miserable. The mortgage payment that looked manageable on paper is squeezing them every single month. They can't afford to furnish the place the way they wanted. They can't go out to dinner. Vacations are out of the question. Every unexpected expense—a car repair, a medical bill, a broken appliance—becomes a crisis.

They're house poor. They own a beautiful home, and they can't afford to enjoy their lives inside it.

I don't want that for you. So let's talk about what you can actually afford—not the maximum a lender will approve, but the amount that lets you buy a home and still live a life you enjoy.

WHY PREAPPROVAL AMOUNTS ARE OFTEN TOO HIGH

When a lender pre-approves you for a mortgage, they're running calculations based on formulas and guidelines. They're looking at your income, your debts, your credit score, current interest rates, and standardized ratios that predict the statistical likelihood of default.

What they're not doing is thinking about your life. Your priorities. Your goals beyond homeownership. Your happiness.

Lending guidelines represent the maximum debt load that statistical models suggest you can carry without defaulting. They're designed to protect the lender from loss. They're not designed to ensure that you'll be comfortable, happy, and financially healthy.

The guidelines say nothing about whether you'll be able to save for retirement. Whether you'll have money for your kids' activities. Whether you'll be able to take a vacation or handle an emergency. Whether you'll actually enjoy living in the home you bought, or whether every single month will feel like walking a financial tightrope.

That's why I tell everyone the same thing. Treat your preapproval amount as an absolute ceiling, not a target. And seriously consider shopping well below that ceiling.

THE 28/36 RULE

The 28/36 rule is a traditional guideline for housing affordability that's been used for decades.

The twenty-eight means your total monthly housing costs—principal, interest, property taxes, homeowner's insurance, and HOA fees if applicable—shouldn't exceed 28 percent of your gross monthly income. If you make $6,000 per month gross, that's a maximum housing payment of $1,680.

The thirty-six means your total monthly debt payments, including housing plus all other debts like car loans, student loans, and minimum credit card payments, shouldn't exceed 36 percent of your gross monthly income. On that same $6,000 income, that's $2,160 total for all debts.

These percentages are based on decades of data about what debt loads people can sustain without serious financial strain. For many families, staying at or below these numbers allows for a reasonably comfortable life.

But here's the important caveat. These guidelines were developed in a different era. Healthcare wasn't as expensive. Childcare costs weren't as crushing. Student loan debt wasn't as prevalent. Retirement savings needs weren't as urgent.

For some families, even staying within traditional guidelines still leaves them feeling stretched. Your situation is unique. Your expenses are unique. Use 28/36 as a starting point for analysis, not as an automatic answer.

THE LIFESTYLE BUDGET EXERCISE

Here's an exercise I walk homebuyers through that changes the way they think about affordability. Instead of starting with a home price and figuring out if you can make it work, you start with the life you want to live and work backward to find the housing number that fits.

Sit down and write out what your ideal month costs beyond housing. Be specific. How much do you want to spend on groceries? Dining out? How much do your kids' activities cost—sports, music lessons, tutoring? What about date nights? Family outings? What does your car cost you each month with the payment, insurance, and gas? How much are you putting toward retirement? What about saving for vacations, even if it's just a little each month? What about gifts for birthdays and holidays? Clothes? Haircuts? The stuff people forget to budget for but spend money on every single month.

Add all of that up. Then add your non-housing debt payments. Then subtract that total from your take-home pay—not your gross income, your actual take-home after taxes and deductions. What's left over is what you can realistically put toward housing each month without sacrificing the life you want to live.

That number might be lower than what the lender approved you for, which is good. That's the honest number. That's the number that keeps you sane, keeps your marriage healthy, and keeps your kids in their activities. That's the number that lets you sleep at night. I'd rather see you buy a home at a price that lets you live your life than one that takes your life over.

Here's something I do personally that I think everyone should try. Before I commit to any higher monthly payment—whether it's a mortgage, a car, or any other loan—I look at my monthly budget, and then I actually live with that higher cost for a few months before I sign anything. I adjust my spending as if I already have that new payment, and the extra money goes straight into a high-yield savings account. If, after a few months, my family is comfortable and we haven't felt squeezed, I know the number works. If it felt tight or stressful, I know I need to adjust before I lock myself into something I can't easily undo.

Think about it this way. If you're going from renting a small one-bedroom or two-bedroom apartment to owning a home, your monthly cost is almost certainly going up. And it should, because the benefits of owning versus renting—building equity, locking in your housing cost, having something that's actually yours—are worth it. But that doesn't mean the jump won't feel different in your day-to-day life. A dry run lets you feel that difference before it's permanent. You get to test-drive the budget and find out if it actually works for you and your family, not just on a spreadsheet but in real life.

And the best part? That money you saved during the dry run is now sitting in a high-yield savings account earning interest. Use it toward your down payment, your closing costs, your move-in expenses, or just keep it growing as your emergency fund. Either way, you come out ahead. You've proven the budget works, and you've built savings doing it.

TWO FAMILIES, TWO OUTCOMES

I've been doing this long enough to see how different buying decisions play out over time, and two families come to mind that tell the story perfectly.

The first family came to me pre-approved for about $380,000. They were excited, and I understood why—that's a lot of house.

They found a home right at the top of their approval and went for it. On paper, the numbers worked. Their DTI was within guidelines. The lender signed off. Everything checked the boxes.

But within six months, they were stressed. The mortgage payment, plus taxes and insurance, was eating up almost everything they brought home. They stopped going out. They stopped saving. When the water heater died, they had to put it on a credit card because they had no cushion left. A home that was supposed to be their dream started feeling like an anchor.

The second family was approved for a similar amount. But they chose to buy about $60,000 below their max. They picked a home they loved in a neighborhood they were happy with, and the monthly payment left room to breathe. They still went on vacation that first year. They still put money into retirement. When their heating, ventilation, and air conditioning (HVAC) system needed repairs, they paid for them out of savings without blinking. Two years later, they were in a stronger financial position than on the day they moved in.

Same income range, same approval amounts, and completely different outcomes. The difference wasn't luck—it was the decision they made about how much house to actually buy.

THE TRUE COST OF HOMEOWNERSHIP

Your monthly mortgage payment is just the beginning. To understand what you can truly afford, you need to account for all the costs of homeownership.

Property taxes vary wildly by location. Two identical houses just a few miles apart but in different tax jurisdictions can have annual tax bills that differ by thousands of dollars. Research property tax rates carefully in areas you're considering.

Lenders require homeowners insurance, which protects your investment. Costs depend on the home's location, construction type, age, your coverage levels, and your chosen deductibles. Get actual quotes for properties you're seriously considering rather than relying on estimates.

I always advise families to shop for their car insurance at the same time they're shopping for homeowner's insurance. Pull out your declaration page—the document that shows your current car insurance coverage—so you can compare apples to apples when you get quotes. Most insurance companies offer a bundle discount when you carry both your home and auto policies with them, which means you should actually save money on your car insurance just by combining the two. It's one of those moves that takes a little effort upfront but puts money back in your pocket every single month.

If you're buying new construction, you may benefit from lower homeowner's insurance costs right out of the gate because everything is new—new roof, new electrical, new plumbing, new HVAC. Insurance companies view that as less risk, and less risk often means lower premiums. That's another advantage of new construction that doesn't always get talked about.

And whether you're buying new or resale, make sure you find out if the property is in a flood zone or if you might need hurricane coverage. Standard homeowner's insurance didn't cover flood damage, and in many coastal or low-lying areas, flood insurance is required by the lender. Hurricane or windstorm coverage may also be a separate policy, depending on your location.

These additional policies can really add up, and if you don't factor them into your budget ahead of time, you're going to get a surprise you didn't plan for.

HOA fees, if you're buying in a community with a homeowners association, can add $100 to $500 or more to your monthly costs. These fees cover shared amenities and exterior maintenance, but they're not optional—you must pay them as long as you own the property.

Maintenance and repairs will cost you. The general rule is roughly 1 percent of your home's value per year (on average). A $300,000 home needs about $3,000 annually—$250 per month—for upkeep. Some years you'll spend less, and others you'll spend much more when a major system fails.

Utilities often increase when you move from an apartment to a house. More square footage means more to heat, cool, and power. A yard might need irrigation. You might have systems to maintain—septic, well, or pool—that apartments didn't require. Budget higher than what you're currently paying, at a minimum.

Add all of these together. That's your real monthly cost of owning a home—not just the mortgage payment, but everything. That's the number you need to be able to afford comfortably.

• • • RESOURCE • • •

If you want help running those numbers, head over to www.justinskeytohomelife.com and use the True Housing Cost Calculator in the Free Home-buying Tools section. I built it specifically for this purpose—so you can see the full picture before you commit, not after.

THE COSTS NOBODY WARNS YOU ABOUT

There's a whole category of expenses that hits new homeowners in the first few months, and almost nobody budgets for them. I want to make sure you're not caught off guard.

Moving costs are obvious, yet people still underestimate them. Whether you're hiring movers or renting a truck and doing it yourself, it adds up fast. Boxes, tape, packing materials, fuel, pizza for the friends who helped you carry the couch—it's rarely less than a few hundred dollars and often much more.

Then there are the immediate purchases. You walk into your new house and realize you need things you never thought about. Blinds or curtains for every window, because your apartment came with them, but your new house doesn't. A lawn mower, because that grass isn't going to cut itself. Garden hoses. A ladder. Basic tools if you don't already have them. Cleaning supplies for a much bigger space. Maybe a second set of trash cans for the garage.

Appliances can be a big one. If the home doesn't come with a refrigerator, washer, or dryer, you're looking at a significant expense right out of the gate. Even if it does come with appliances, they might be older units that need replacing sooner than you'd like.

And then there's furniture. Your apartment furniture might not fill a house. Rooms that looked fine in the listing photos look empty when you're standing in them with nothing but a couch and a TV. You don't have to furnish everything at once—and I'd strongly recommend that you don't—but the temptation is real, and it's easy to blow through thousands of dollars in the first few weeks trying to make the place feel like home.

Budget for these things before you close. Set aside a separate fund—even $1,000 to $2,000—specifically for move-in costs.

It won't cover everything, but it will keep you from putting it all on credit cards and starting your homeownership journey in a deeper hole than you planned.

STRESS TESTING YOUR BUDGET

Before committing to a housing budget, stress-test it against realistic scenarios.

What if interest rates rise before you lock in? Rates can move significantly between preapproval and closing. If you're shopping at the very top of your budget based on today's rates, a rate increase could push you over the edge. Can you still afford it at a rate a point or two higher than today's?

What if property taxes get reassessed significantly higher after you buy? Many areas reassess property values after sales, and your taxes might increase substantially from what the current owner pays. Are you prepared for that?

What if you need a new roof or HVAC system in year two? Major systems fail. Sometimes you get a warning, and sometimes you don't. Can your budget handle a $10,000 or $15,000 emergency expense without going into debt?

What if one income goes away temporarily? Job loss, illness, parental leave, family emergency—these things happen. Would you still be able to make the mortgage payment on one income, even if only for a few months?

A budget that survives these stress tests is a budget you can commit to with confidence. A budget that crumbles under any pressure is a warning sign that you're stretching too far.

FINDING YOUR COMFORT ZONE

I know this approach might mean buying less house than you dreamed of. I know it might mean a longer commute, a different neighborhood, or fewer bedrooms than you wanted. I know it might feel like settling.

But it also means buying a home that brings you joy instead of stress. A home that's a blessing, not a burden. A home where you can actually live your life, not just make mortgage payments.

I've seen both outcomes. I've helped families who stretched too far and regretted it for years. And I've helped families who bought within their means and never looked back.

The second group is happier—every single time.

Trust the process. Run the numbers honestly. Find the price point where you can be a homeowner and still live the life you want—still have date nights, still take vacations, still save for retirement, and still sleep soundly at night.

That's the real dream. Not just owning a home, but owning a home that makes your life better instead of harder.

•••KEY TAKEAWAY•••

The bank will approve you for more than you should spend. Just because you qualify for a $400,000 mortgage didn't mean you should take it. Leave room in your budget for other aspects of life—vacations, emergencies, kids' activities, retirement savings. A house that makes you house poor isn't a dream home.

CHAPTER 7
The Hidden Costs Nobody Tells You About

• • •

In my nearly three decades in the housing industry, one of the things I take the most pride in is making sure my families know exactly what to expect before they sign anything—no surprises, no fine print they didn't understand, and no phone calls six months later asking why nobody told them about this cost or that fee. I prepare my buyers for everything, because that's what they deserve.

But I also know that not every buyer has someone in their corner doing that for them. Too many families budget for homeownership, focusing solely on the mortgage payment, only to find out the hard way that the purchase price and monthly note are just part of the picture. That's why I'm dedicating a full chapter to this topic.

And I want to be clear about something right up front. This chapter isn't here to scare you out of buying a home. Not even close. Homeownership is one of the best decisions you can make for your family's future, and I believe that with everything I have. This chapter exists so you go in prepared, just as I prepare every family I work with. The families who struggle aren't the ones who face unexpected costs—every homeowner faces those. The ones who struggle are the ones who didn't see them coming. You're going to see them coming.

CLOSING COSTS: THE FIRST SURPRISE

As discussed previously, your down payment isn't the only cash you'll need to bring to the closing table. There's also a substantial bill for closing costs—fees and expenses that typically run 2 to 5 percent of your loan amount. On a $300,000 mortgage, that's $6,000 to $15,000 on top of your down payment.

What do these costs cover? Lender fees include loan origination, underwriting, processing, and various administrative charges. Third-party fees include appraisal, credit report, title search, title insurance, survey, and other services the lender requires. Government fees include recording your deed and mortgage, as well as any applicable transfer taxes. Prepaid items include your first year of homeowner's insurance, initial deposits into your escrow account for taxes and insurance, and prepaid interest from closing until your first payment date.

Your lender is required to provide a "loan estimate" within three business days of your application, detailing expected closing costs. Read it carefully. Ask questions about anything you don't understand. Compare estimates from different lenders, as fees can vary significantly.

Some closing costs are negotiable. Shop around for title insurance and settlement services. Ask lenders about fee waivers or credits. In some situations, you can negotiate for the seller to contribute toward your closing costs as part of the purchase agreement. And as I mentioned earlier, many builders will cover all closing costs when you use their preferred lender and title company. The point is, this number isn't set in stone—do your homework, and you can bring it down.

THE ONGOING COSTS OF HOMEOWNERSHIP

Once you've closed, the costs keep coming. Some are predictable, while others catch you by surprise. But here's what I want you to remember as we go through these. Every one of these costs is an investment in something you own. When you were renting, your landlord collected your rent money and kept the property. Now that money is going toward a home that's yours.

Property taxes are usually paid through escrow—your lender collects a portion each month and pays the bill when it's due. Tax rates can change, and properties are sometimes reassessed after a sale, so your taxes might be higher than what the previous owner paid. Budget conservatively. But also remember that property taxes fund the schools, roads, and services that make your neighborhood a good place to live—and in many cases, those taxes are deductible on your federal return.

Insurance costs can increase over time due to inflation and changing risk assessments. But insurance protects the biggest investment most families will ever make. Shop for insurance regularly, bundle your home and auto policies for discounts, and ask about any available credits for features like security systems, smoke detectors, or a newer roof.

HOA fees, if applicable, typically increase annually. But consider what you get for those fees—community amenities, exterior maintenance, landscaping, snow removal, sometimes even water or trash service. Review the HOA's financials and fee history before buying, and watch for special assessments. A well-run HOA maintains adequate reserves and keeps surprises to a minimum.

Utilities in a house are almost always higher than in an apartment. More space to heat and cool, a yard that needs water, maybe a pool pump or outdoor lighting. Budget 20 to 50 percent more than you currently pay. But you're also in control now—you can upgrade to energy-efficient appliances, add insulation, install a smart thermostat, and actually see the savings on your own bill instead of padding your landlord's bottom line.

MAINTENANCE: INVESTING IN WHAT'S YOURS

This is the one that catches people off guard—the ongoing cost of keeping a house in good condition. The general rule is to budget 1 percent of your home's value annually for maintenance and repairs. A $300,000 home needs about $3,000 per year—$250 per month—for upkeep.

Some years you'll spend less, like changing some air filters, doing some basic lawn care, and handling minor repairs. No big deal. In other years, the HVAC system fails, or the water heater dies. These aren't unusual events—they're part of owning a home. Every system has a lifespan, and everything eventually needs attention.

But there's a difference between this and renting. Every dollar you put into maintaining your home protects and often increases its value. A new roof isn't just a bill—it's an investment that adds value to your property and keeps it marketable. Replacing an aging HVAC system makes your home more efficient and more attractive to future buyers. When you were renting, your maintenance dollars went to your landlord's asset. Now they go to yours.

Build that maintenance fund before you need it. Treat it as a non-negotiable monthly expense, just like your mortgage payment. When something breaks—and eventually something will—you'll handle it calmly instead of scrambling for a credit card.

THE NEW-CONSTRUCTION ADVANTAGE

This is a good place to talk about one of the reasons I'm such a believer in new construction, especially for first-time buyers. It saves you real money in the early years of homeownership when your budget is at its tightest.

When everything in your home is brand-new—the roof, the HVAC, the plumbing, the electrical, the appliances—your maintenance costs in those first several years are going to be minimal. You're not inheriting someone else's aging water heater or a furnace that's on its last legs. Everything is fresh, everything is under warranty, and that means your maintenance fund has time to grow before you ever need to tap into it in a meaningful way.

Insurance is another area where new construction works in your favor. Insurance companies assess risk, and a brand-new home with modern materials, updated building codes, and new systems is lower risk than a resale home with a fifteen-year-old roof and outdated wiring. That lower risk often translates into lower premiums, which puts money back in your pocket every single month.

And then there's energy efficiency. New-construction homes are built to current energy codes, which are significantly more stringent than what was required even ten or fifteen years ago.

Better insulation, tighter building envelopes, high-efficiency HVAC systems, Energy Star appliances, low-emissivity (low-E) windows—all of this adds up to lower utility bills from day one. I've seen families move from older resale homes into new constructions and cut their energy costs by 30 percent or more. Over the course of a year, that's hundreds of dollars in savings that go right back into your budget.

When you add it all up—lower maintenance, lower insurance, lower utilities—new construction can save you thousands of dollars in those critical first years of ownership. That's money that stays in your pocket, builds your emergency fund, or goes toward making your new house feel like home. It's one of the smartest moves a first-time buyer can make.

MOVING AND SETUP COSTS

Moving into a new home generates its own set of expenses. Professional movers can run several hundred to a few thousand dollars. Even if you move yourself, there are truck rentals, packing supplies, and probably pizza for whoever helps you carry the couch.

Setup costs include utility deposits, internet installation, and changing the locks for security. Then there are the immediate purchases—window treatments, basic tools, a lawn mower if you're coming from an apartment, garden hoses, and cleaning supplies for a bigger space.

Build a move-in budget separate from your down payment and closing costs. Even setting aside $1,000 to $2,000 specifically for this purpose helps you avoid starting homeownership with new credit card debt. And don't feel like you have to do everything at once. The house will still be there next month. Prioritize what you need now and spread the rest out over time.

THE LIFESTYLE CREEP TRAP

Here's a subtler cost to watch for—the pressure to upgrade everything once you own a home. Your apartment furniture looks different in the new living room. The deck needs outdoor furniture. The garage feels empty. The guest bathroom could use an update.

None of these is urgent. All of them cost money. And the list never ends. I've seen new homeowners blow through thousands in the first few months trying to make everything perfect right away, which puts them in a hole they didn't need to be in.

My advice? Live in your house for a while before you start changing things. Figure out what you actually need versus what you just want. And budget for improvements over time instead of financing everything at once. Your home doesn't have to be a magazine cover on day one. It just has to be yours.

THE FINANCIAL BENEFITS NOBODY TALKS ABOUT ENOUGH

For all the costs we just covered, there's a side of the equation that doesn't get enough attention: the financial benefits that come with owning a home.

Mortgage interest is tax-deductible for many homeowners. Depending on your tax situation, this can put thousands of dollars back in your pocket every year, especially in the early years of your loan when most of your payment goes toward interest. Property taxes are often deductible as well. These deductions can make a meaningful difference when you file your return, and for a lot of families, the tax savings alone offset a significant portion of those "hidden costs" we just discussed.

And when you eventually sell your home, the IRS allows you to exclude up to $250,000 in capital gains from taxes if you're single, or $500,000 if you're married filing jointly, as long as you've lived in the home for at least two of the last five years. That's profit you keep. Try finding that kind of tax advantage anywhere else.

THE EQUITY PAYOFF

Here's the part that makes all of these costs worth it. Every single mortgage payment builds equity, which is the difference between what your home is worth and what you still owe on it. Every month, that gap gets wider in your favor.

Five years into homeownership, you've built real wealth that renters simply never will. Your home has likely appreciated in value while your loan balance has gone down. That combination means your net worth is growing from two directions at once. Meanwhile, the family still renting has paid five years of someone else's mortgage and has nothing to show for it.

That equity isn't just a number on paper. It's options. It's the ability to borrow against your home for improvements or emergencies. It's a stronger financial position when you're ready to move up. It's generational wealth you can pass to your children. It's the foundation my Mom never had but worked so hard to give us the chance to build.

HOMEOWNER HACKS TO SAVE MONEY

One of the best things about being a homeowner is that you don't have to pay someone for every little thing. Learning basic do-it-yourself (DIY) skills can save you hundreds or even thousands of dollars a year. Changing a faucet, replacing a light fixture, patching drywall, caulking a bathtub—these aren't complicated jobs, and there's a YouTube video for just about every one of them.

Seasonal maintenance is another money saver. Clean your gutters in the fall, service your HVAC before summer and winter, check your weatherstripping, and inspect your roof after storms. These small efforts prevent the expensive surprises. A $20 air filter changed on schedule can save you $5,000 in HVAC replacement costs down the road.

If you want peace of mind in those early years, consider a home warranty. For a few hundred dollars a year, a warranty covers repair or replacement of major systems and appliances. It's not perfect—read the fine print and understand the limitations—but for new homeowners who don't yet have a fat maintenance fund, it can be a smart safety net.

• • • RESOURCE • • •

If you want more tips on saving money, tackling projects, and building a great home life, follow along at www.justinskeytohomelife.com. I share practical advice on my blog and social media channels on everything from home maintenance to making the most of your space. My goal is to help you not just buy a home but actually enjoy living in it. While you're there, check out the Free Home-buying Tools section. I built a True Housing Cost Calculator that lets you plug in all of these numbers—mortgage, taxes, insurance, maintenance, utilities, everything—so you can see the full picture before you commit. No surprises. Just clarity.

PREPARED, NOT SCARED

I know this chapter covered a lot of costs. But I hope you're walking away feeling prepared, not discouraged. Every homeowner faces these expenses. The ones who thrive are the ones who planned for them. You now know more about the true cost of homeownership than most people learn in their first five years of owning. That knowledge is power, and it's going to serve you well.

Homeownership is still one of the best things you can do for your family. The stability, the equity, the tax benefits, the pride of having something that's truly yours—none of that goes away because of maintenance costs or closing fees. Those are just part of the deal. And now that you know about them, they won't catch you off guard. You're ready.

•••JUSTIN'S TIP•••

Budget an extra $5,000 to $10,000 beyond your down payment and closing costs for first-year expenses. Every new homeowner discovers things they need to buy, fix, or replace. Having this cushion prevents you from putting it all on credit cards.

CHAPTER 8
GETTING PRE-APPROVED

• • •

EVERYTHING WE'VE COVERED IN Part One has been building toward this moment. The financial assessment. The credit work. The debt management. The saving. The budgeting. All of it has been preparation for the step that transforms you from someone who wants to buy a home to someone who can.

Getting pre-approved for a mortgage is when preparation meets opportunity. It's when all that background work becomes a credential that opens doors. In competitive markets, sellers won't even look at offers from buyers who aren't pre-approved. A preapproval letter is your proof that you're serious, capable, and ready to move forward.

But it's more than just a piece of paper to wave at sellers. The pre-approval process forces you to confront exactly where you stand. It surfaces any remaining issues that need to be addressed. It gives you a real, verified number to shop with instead of a guess.

Let's make sure you're ready for it.

PREQUALIFICATION VS. PREAPPROVAL

These two terms get thrown around interchangeably, but they mean very different things.

Prequalification is a quick, preliminary estimate based on the information you provide, typically through a brief conversation or an online form. The lender hasn't verified anything. They haven't pulled your credit report. They haven't confirmed your income or employment. They're just giving you a rough guess at what you might qualify for based on what you've told them.

A prequalification letter is worth very little. Sellers know it's basically meaningless. It doesn't prove you can actually get a loan—it just says that if everything you claimed is true, you might qualify. That's not the same thing at all.

Preapproval is much more rigorous. The lender actually pulls your credit. They verify your income and employment through documentation. They review your assets and debts. They run your numbers through their underwriting criteria. What they give you at the end is a conditional commitment to lend you a specific amount, subject to finding a suitable property and completing final verification.

A preapproval letter has real weight. Sellers take it seriously because they know you've been vetted. It strengthens your offers and makes your position more credible.

Always get fully pre-approved, not just pre-qualified. Don't waste time with anything less.

DOCUMENTS YOU'LL NEED

The preapproval process requires extensive documentation. Having everything organized before you start saves time and frustration.

You'll need identification—a driver's license and a Social Security card. You'll need proof of income—recent pay stubs, usually thirty days' worth, W-2 forms for the past two years, and tax returns if you're self-employed or have significant non-wage income. You'll need bank statements for all accounts—usually the most recent two or three months, and all pages, even blank ones. You'll need statements for retirement accounts and other assets you want counted toward reserves.

If you have other debts, bring documentation for them as well—student loan statements, car loan contracts, and credit card statements. The lender will see these on your credit report anyway, but having details handy speeds up the process.

If you've had credit issues in the past, be prepared to explain them. Late payments, collections, bankruptcies, foreclosures—have dates and circumstances ready. A brief written explanation of what happened and what you've done since can help underwriters understand your situation.

If any of your down payment is coming from gift funds, get your gift letter ready. The donor will need to provide a letter stating the amount, their relationship to you, that no repayment is expected, and documentation of the source of the funds.

Gather everything before you apply. Missing documents create delays.

CHOOSING A LENDER

Not all lenders are the same, and the one you choose matters more than most people realize.

Get quotes from at least three different lenders. Include a mix of types—maybe a big national bank, a local credit union, and an online lender or mortgage broker. Each type has potential advantages: big banks offer familiarity and branch access; credit unions often have competitive rates for members; online lenders may have lower overhead and faster processes; and mortgage brokers can shop multiple lenders for you.

Compare not just interest rates but also fees, closing costs, and responsiveness. A slightly lower rate isn't worth much if the lender is impossible to reach or misses deadlines.

Rate shopping within a short window—typically fourteen to forty-five days, depending on the scoring model—counts as a single inquiry for credit scoring purposes. Don't let fear of credit pulls stop you from comparing options. The difference between lenders can be tens of thousands of dollars over the life of your loan.

Pay attention to communication. Is the loan officer responsive? Do they explain things clearly? Do they seem genuinely interested in helping you, or are you just another file to process? How quickly do they return calls and emails?

The lowest rate isn't always the best deal. A lender who's responsive, competent, and actually helpful can be worth paying slightly more for. The cheapest option that can't close on time or creates problems during the process costs you in other ways.

WHAT HAPPENS DURING PREAPPROVAL

Once you've chosen a lender and submitted your documentation, they'll verify everything. They'll confirm your employment directly with your employer. They'll review your bank statements for any large deposits or unusual activity that needs explanation. They'll calculate your DTI and verify that your credit profile matches what you've represented.

If everything checks out, you'll receive a preapproval letter stating the loan amount you qualify for, subject to finding a suitable property and completing final verification. The letter is typically valid for sixty to ninety days.

If there are issues—maybe your credit score is lower than you thought, maybe there's an old collection you didn't know about, maybe your DTI is higher than acceptable—the lender will let you know. This is actually valuable information. Better to discover problems now, when you can address them, than when you're trying to close on a house.

PREAPPROVAL AND NEW CONSTRUCTION

If you're buying a new-construction home, the preapproval process works a little differently, and I want to make sure you know what to expect so you don't get anxious during the build.

When you get pre-approved and go under contract on a home that's being built, there's often a gap of several months between your initial preapproval and when the home is ready to close. During that time, it's completely normal not to hear much from your lender. That silence can feel unsettling—you're making the biggest purchase of your life, and nobody's calling you about the loan. But don't panic. That's how it works.

Your lender knows the home is being built. They're waiting for the builder to notify them that your home is approximately thirty to forty-five days from completion. That's when the lender kicks back into gear. They'll reach out to you, start collecting updated documentation—fresh pay stubs, recent bank statements, updated employment verification—and they'll pull your credit again to make sure everything is still in good standing.

This is why the advice I'm about to give you in the next section is so critically important. That second credit pull is coming, and your financial picture needs to look the same or better than it did during your initial preapproval. If something has changed for the worse, you could have a serious problem right when you're about to get the keys to your new home.

Be patient during the build. Trust the process. Stay in touch with your sales manager if you have questions about the construction timeline, and know that your lender will re-engage when the time is right.

PROTECTING YOUR PREAPPROVAL

This section might be the most important guidance I write in this entire chapter, and I need you to take it seriously. Once you're pre-approved, whether you're buying new construction, resale, or anything in between, protect that approval like your home depends on it—because it does.

Your preapproval is based on a snapshot of your financial situation at a specific point in time. If that picture changes significantly between preapproval and closing, your approval can be revoked. I've seen it happen, and it's devastating.

Don't open new credit accounts. Don't make large purchases on credit. Don't finance a car. Don't change jobs or income sources if you can avoid it. Don't make large deposits that you can't document the source of. Don't co-sign loans for anyone else. Keep your financial life as stable and boring as possible until you have keys in your hand.

And I need to warn you about something specific, because I've seen this go wrong more than once in my career. As you near closing, furniture companies and appliance stores will try to get you to open a line of credit so you can have everything ready for move-in day. Some of them will tell you it's just a "soft pull" on your credit—that it won't affect your score. Don't trust this. I've had families during my career who lost their house at the last minute because they didn't follow my advice on this. They allowed a company to run their credit, thinking it was a soft pull, but it turned out to be a hard inquiry that dropped their score below the approvable guidelines. Just like that, the loan fell apart right at the finish line.

I can't stress this enough. Don't apply for any new credit—furniture, appliances, credit cards, store accounts, nothing—until you're physically handed the keys to your home. Not when you're "pretty sure" you're going to close. Not when someone tells you it won't matter. Not until those keys are in your hand. Period.

If a change is truly necessary—you need a new car because yours broke down, you're facing a job change you can't avoid, or some other major financial event comes up—talk to your lender first before you do anything. Let them tell you how it will affect your loan and whether it's safe to proceed. A five-minute phone call can save you from losing everything you've worked for.

WHAT PREAPPROVAL MEANS—AND WHAT IT DOESN'T

Preapproval means a lender has verified your information and is willing to make you a loan, subject to finding a suitable property and completing final verification. It's a significant milestone.

But it's not a guarantee. The approval is conditional. If you lose your job, if your credit score drops, if the property doesn't appraise at the purchase price, if title issues emerge, if something material changes—the loan can still fall through.

Treat preapproval as a green light to start shopping seriously, not as a done deal. Keep your finances stable. Stay in communication with your lender. Don't count on anything until you're actually sitting at the closing table with keys in your hand.

With your preapproval letter in hand, you've completed the foundation work. The preparation phase is over. You know where you stand financially, you've addressed credit issues, you've managed debt, you've saved your down payment, you understand what you can truly afford, and you have a lender ready to work with you.

Now comes the exciting part. Let's find your home.

• • • WATCH OUT • • •

Don't make big financial changes after preapproval. Don't change jobs, open new credit cards, make large purchases, move money around, or co-sign for anyone. Any of these can derail your approval. Stay financially "boring" until you have the keys in your hand.

• • •

PREAPPROVAL DOCUMENT CHECKLIST

• • •

- ☐ Pay stubs (most recent thirty days)
- ☐ W-2 forms (past two years)
- ☐ Tax returns (past two years)—all pages
- ☐ Bank statements—all accounts (past two to three months)
- ☐ Investment and retirement account statements
- ☐ Government-issued photo identification
- ☐ Social Security card or number
- ☐ Current address and two-year address history
- ☐ Landlord contact information

PART TWO
FINDING YOUR HOME

CHAPTERS 9–14

THE RIGHT HOME IS OUT THERE.
NOW YOU'RE READY TO FIND IT.

CHAPTER 9

UNDERSTANDING YOUR LOAN OPTIONS

• • •

THE MORTGAGE YOU CHOOSE will be with you for a long time—fifteen years, thirty years, maybe even longer if you refinance and restart the clock. The terms you accept will determine your monthly payment, the total interest you pay over the life of the loan, and how quickly you build equity in your home.

This isn't a decision to make casually. Understanding your options matters more than most people realize. A slightly better rate or a more appropriate loan type can mean tens of thousands of dollars over time.

I'm going to walk you through the major loan types, explain how they work, and help you think about which might be right for your specific situation. This isn't about memorizing every detail—it's about understanding enough to have informed conversations with lenders and make choices that serve your long-term interests.

CONVENTIONAL LOANS

Conventional loans are mortgages that a government agency doesn't back. They're the most common type of home loan and come with a wide range of options for different situations.

To qualify for a conventional loan, you typically need a credit score of at least 620, though higher scores qualify you for better rates. You need a documented, stable income and a debt-to-income (DTI) ratio that falls within guidelines—usually 43 percent or less for the back-end ratio. However, some programs allow higher with compensating factors.

Down payment requirements vary. You can put down as little as 3 percent with some programs designed for first-time buyers, though 5 to 20 percent is more common. If you put down less than 20 percent, you'll pay private mortgage insurance (PMI) until you reach 20 percent equity—either through payments or appreciation.

Conventional loans come in two main varieties: conforming and non-conforming. Conforming loans meet the guidelines set by Fannie Mae and Freddie Mac, government-sponsored enterprises that buy mortgages from lenders. These guidelines include maximum loan amounts that vary by location—higher in expensive markets, lower elsewhere. Non-conforming loans, often called jumbo loans, exceed these limits and typically have stricter requirements because they pose greater risk to lenders.

The advantage of conventional loans is flexibility. There are options for various situations, competitive rates for those with strong credit, and PMI that can be removed once you build sufficient equity. The disadvantage is that the qualification requirements are relatively strict compared to those of some government-backed alternatives.

ZERO-DOWN PORTFOLIO LOANS

I touched on this in an earlier chapter, but it belongs here, too, because this is where you're comparing all your options. Some community banks and credit unions offer zero-down conventional portfolio loans that they keep on their own books rather than sell to Fannie Mae or Freddie Mac. Because they set their own rules, these programs can offer benefits you won't find with standard conventional loans.

We're talking zero down payment, no PMI, and in many cases a below-market interest rate—sometimes with no income cap. These aren't widely advertised, and you usually have to walk into a local bank or credit union and ask specifically about portfolio loan products to find them. But if you qualify, the savings can be substantial. No PMI alone can save you hundreds of dollars a month compared to a conventional loan with less than 20 percent down.

Don't limit your search to the big national lenders. Some of the best loan products I've seen my home buyers take advantage of came from institutions most people have never heard of.

FEDERAL HOUSING ADMINISTRATION (FHA) LOANS

FHA loans are mortgages insured by the Federal Housing Administration, a government agency within the Department of Housing and Urban Development. They're designed to make homeownership accessible to people who might not qualify for conventional financing.

The biggest advantage is more flexible qualification requirements. You can qualify with a credit score as low as 580 and just 3.5 percent down, or as low as 500 if you can put down 10 percent.

DTI ratios can exceed conventional limits in some cases, especially when compensating factors are present. Recent credit events, such as bankruptcy or foreclosure, have shorter waiting periods than conventional loans do.

The trade-off is mortgage insurance. FHA loans require both an upfront mortgage insurance premium—currently 1.75 percent of the loan amount, which can be rolled into the loan—and an annual premium paid monthly. Unlike PMI on conventional loans, FHA mortgage insurance doesn't automatically drop off when you reach 20 percent equity. If you put down less than 10 percent, you pay a mortgage insurance premium (MIP) for the life of the loan.

FHA loans make sense for buyers with lower credit scores, limited down payments, or other factors that make conventional qualification difficult. But if you can qualify for conventional financing, compare the total costs carefully—sometimes FHA's mortgage insurance structure makes it more expensive over time.

VETERANS AFFAIRS (VA) LOANS

VA loans are mortgages guaranteed by the Department of Veterans Affairs, available to eligible active-duty service members, veterans, National Guard and Reserve members, and some surviving spouses.

If you've served and are eligible, VA loans offer remarkable benefits that are hard to match elsewhere. No down payment required—you can finance 100 percent of the purchase price. No monthly mortgage insurance, despite the zero-down feature. Competitive interest rates, often lower than conventional loans. More flexible credit requirements and DTI ratios. Limits on closing costs that can be charged to veterans.

There's a funding fee, which helps sustain the program for future veterans. The fee varies based on your service history, down payment amount, and whether you've used a VA loan before. It can be rolled into the loan amount. Some veterans with service-connected disabilities are exempt from the funding fee entirely.

If you've earned VA eligibility through your service, seriously consider using it. It's one of the best mortgage products available, and it's a benefit you've earned.

US DEPARTMENT OF AGRICULTURE (USDA) LOANS

USDA loans are mortgages guaranteed by the US Department of Agriculture, designed to promote homeownership in rural and some suburban areas.

Like VA loans, USDA loans require no down payment—100 percent financing is available. There's a guarantee fee, both upfront and annual, but these are typically lower than FHA mortgage insurance premiums.

The catch is the eligibility requirements. The property must be in a USDA-eligible area, and you need to meet income limits that vary by location and household size. If you're considering properties in less urbanized areas and your income falls within limits, check USDA eligibility. The zero-down feature and competitive rates make it worth exploring.

FIXED-RATE VS. ADJUSTABLE-RATE MORTGAGES

Beyond the type of loan, you'll choose between fixed and adjustable interest rates.

Fixed-rate mortgages lock in your interest rate for the entire loan term. Whether you choose fifteen years, twenty years, thirty years, or another term, your principal and interest payment never changes. This predictability makes budgeting easier and protects you if rates rise significantly during your ownership.

Adjustable-rate mortgages (ARMs) start with a fixed rate for an initial period—commonly five, seven, or ten years—then adjust periodically based on market conditions. The initial rate is typically lower than that of fixed-rate options, resulting in lower payments during that initial period. But they carry risk—if rates rise significantly and you can't refinance or sell, your payments could increase substantially.

For most buyers, especially first-timers planning to stay in their home long-term, fixed-rate mortgages provide peace of mind that's usually worth more than potential savings from an ARM. You know exactly what your principal and interest payment will be for the entire term. That certainty has real value.

RATE BUYDOWNS

A rate buydown is when someone pays upfront to temporarily or permanently reduce the mortgage interest rate. This is a big deal, especially in new construction, because builders frequently offer buydowns as incentives to attract buyers.

A permanent buydown works like discount points, where money is paid at closing to lower your rate for the life of the loan. A temporary buydown reduces your rate for the first one, two, or three years, then it steps up to the full rate. The most common temporary buydown is a two-to-one buydown: your rate is 2 percent below the note rate in year one, 1 percent below in year two, and then the full rate from year three on.

For a first-time buyer, a temporary buydown can be a real advantage. It gives you lower payments in those early years when you're adjusting to the costs of homeownership—buying furniture, building your maintenance fund, settling in. By the time your payment steps up, you've had a couple of years to get your feet under you financially.

Builders love offering buydowns because it makes their homes more attractive without lowering the sale price. Ask about it. If a builder is offering to pay closing costs through their preferred lender, ask whether a rate buydown is available instead or in addition. It never hurts to ask, and the savings over those first couple of years can be significant.

LOCKING YOUR RATE

Once you've found your home and are moving forward with a lender, you'll need to decide when to lock your interest rate. A rate lock guarantees your rate for a specific period—typically thirty to sixty days. However, longer locks are available, especially for new construction, where the build timeline may be several months out.

Timing matters. If you lock and rates drop, you're stuck with the higher rate unless your lender offers a float-down option, which allows you to take advantage of lower rates if they drop by a certain amount after you've locked. Not all lenders offer this, so ask about it upfront. If you don't lock in rates and rates rise, your payment goes up, and your purchasing power goes down.

For new construction with a longer build timeline, talk to your lender about extended rate locks. Some lenders offer locks of 90, 120, or even 180 days or more, though longer locks may come with a slightly higher rate or an upfront fee. It's a trade-off between certainty and cost, and your lender can help you weigh the options based on current market conditions and your expected closing date.

My general advice? If you're happy with the rate and it fits your budget, lock it in. Trying to time the market and wait for rates to drop is a gamble, and I've seen more people get burned waiting than benefit.

POINTS, FEES, AND ANNUAL PERCENTAGE RATE (APR)

When comparing loan offers, look beyond just the interest rate. The full picture includes points, fees, and APR.

Discount points let you pay upfront to reduce your interest rate—essentially prepaying interest. Each point typically costs 1 percent of the loan amount and reduces your rate by about 0.25 percent, though this varies. This can make sense if you're staying in the home long enough for monthly savings to exceed the upfront cost, but run the numbers carefully for your specific situation.

Origination fees, underwriting fees, processing fees, and various other lender charges can vary significantly between lenders. A loan with a slightly higher rate but lower fees might cost less overall than a low-rate loan with heftier fees.

The APR incorporates certain fees in the rate calculation to facilitate comparison, but it's imperfect. The best comparison is the total cost over your expected ownership period. How much will you pay in total—including all fees, points, and interest—if you keep the loan for five years, ten years, or the full term? That's the number that really matters.

• • • RESOURCE • • •

If you want help running these comparisons, head over to www.justinskeytohomelife.com and use the free mortgage calculators in the Free Home-buying Tools section. I built them so you can plug in different scenarios side by side and see exactly what each option costs you.

YOUR LOAN DOESN'T HAVE TO BE FOREVER

Here's something to keep in mind as you make this decision. The loan you start with doesn't have to be the loan you keep forever. If interest rates drop significantly after you buy, refinancing is always an option. You can replace your current mortgage with a new one at a lower rate, potentially saving hundreds of dollars a month.

I've seen buyers stress themselves out trying to find the absolute perfect loan in a high-rate environment, sometimes delaying their purchase for months or years waiting for rates to come down. Meanwhile, home prices kept climbing, and they ended up paying more for the house than they would have if they'd just bought when they were ready.

There's a saying in the housing industry of "marry the house, date the rate." Buy the right home when you're financially ready, and if rates improve down the road, refinance into better terms. You get the home you want now and the rate you want later.

FEATURE	CONVENTIONAL	FHA	VA	USDA
MINIMUM DOWN PAYMENT	3%–5%	3.5%	0%	0%
MINIMUM CREDIT SCORE	620–680	580	VARIES	640
MORTGAGE INSURANCE	IF <20% DOWN	REQUIRED	NONE	REQUIRED
BEST FOR	STRONG CREDIT	LOWER CREDIT	VETERANS	RURAL AREAS

Table 3: Mortgage Loan Type Comparison at a Glance

•••KEY TAKEAWAY•••

FHA loans aren't just for first-time buyers or low-income borrowers. They're for anyone who qualifies. Don't let pride push you toward a conventional loan if FHA is a better fit. The goal is homeownership—use whatever program gets you there.

CHAPTER 10

New Construction vs. Existing Homes

• • •

I've spent nearly three decades in the housing industry, working with both new construction and resale homes. I've seen the quality that good builders deliver. I've watched families fall in love with homes customized to their exact preferences. I know the value of modern building codes, energy efficiency, and warranty protection that comes with new construction. And I've also helped plenty of families find the perfect existing home that checked every box they needed.

But I also know that new construction isn't right for everyone. And you deserve an honest comparison, not a sales pitch.

Both paths—new construction and existing homes—have real advantages and real drawbacks. The right choice depends on your priorities, your timeline, your budget, and what matters most to your family. Let me walk you through both sides so you can make an informed decision.

THE CASE FOR NEW CONSTRUCTION

When you buy new construction, you're the first family to live in that home. No one else's wear and tear. No previous owner's deferred maintenance or questionable repairs. No wondering what's hidden behind the walls. Everything is clean, fresh, and new.

New homes are built to current building codes, which are more stringent than in previous decades—especially regarding energy efficiency, electrical systems, safety features, and structural integrity. Modern insulation, high-efficiency windows, updated HVAC systems, and Energy Star appliances mean lower utility bills and a smaller environmental footprint. Many new homes include smart-home features as standard.

Warranties provide protection that existing homes don't offer. Builders typically provide a one-year warranty for defective work and materials, two years for mechanical systems such as plumbing and electrical, and ten years for structural elements. If something goes wrong during those periods, the builder is responsible for fixing it—not you.

Customization is another significant advantage. Depending on when you buy in the construction process, you might select your lot, floor plan, exterior elevation, and interior finishes. You can choose flooring, countertops, cabinet styles, paint colors, and various upgrades. The home reflects your taste rather than someone else's choices that you have to live with or pay to change.

And there's something emotionally significant about having firsts: cooking the first dinners in that kitchen, celebrating the first holidays in that living room, and making the first memories in those bedrooms. You're not inheriting someone else's history—you're creating your own from scratch.

NOT ALL BUILDERS ARE THE SAME

If you decide new construction is the right path, there's one more thing I need you to understand. The builder you choose matters just as much as the home you choose. Not all builders are the same, and differences among them can significantly affect the quality of your home, the level of personalization you receive, and the overall experience.

In my experience, new construction generally falls into four building models, and understanding them will help you know what to expect before you ever walk into a sales office.

The first is the "spec home" model. The builder selects everything—floor plan, finishes, colors, fixtures—and builds the home before a buyer is ever involved. You're buying what's already been built or what's already been decided. There are no choices to make because every decision has already been made for you. This is the fastest path to moving in, but it offers zero personalization.

The second is the "package selection" model. The builder offers a limited set of pre-designed combinations. You might choose from four cabinet colors, for example, but each cabinet color is bundled with a specific countertop, flooring, and other finishes that have already been paired. You're choosing Package A, Package B, or Package C—not selecting individual finishes. This gives you some variety, but you're still working within tightly controlled options.

The third model lets buyers select all the finishes in the home independently—your cabinets, countertops, flooring, fixtures, tile, and hardware—each chosen separately based on your taste, not a prepackaged bundle. These builders also typically offer predetermined structural options, such as bump-outs, additions, or bonus rooms, that you can add to the base floor plan. You're genuinely designing your home within an established framework.

The fourth is "full custom." You start with a floor plan and can modify nearly everything—moving walls, changing room sizes, adjusting layouts—as long as it works with engineering and structural requirements. Every finish, every detail, you choose every element of the home. This is the most personalized experience and typically the longest timeline, but the result is a home built exactly to your vision.

None of these models is inherently better or worse—it depends on what matters to you. If speed and simplicity are your priority, a spec home gets you in fast. If you want some say but don't need to control every detail, the package model is a good fit. But if personalizing your home is important to you, look for builders operating in that third or fourth category. Throughout my career, I've chosen to work exclusively with builders who offer those latter levels of customization because I believe families deserve a real voice in how their homes are built.

Beyond the selection model, it's worth examining how different builders approach construction.

Some builders—particularly local builders with deep roots in the communities where they build—often exceed minimum building code in ways that make a real difference in how your home performs and holds up over time. Where code may require a specific insulation value, a quality builder may exceed it because they know it results in a better home. Some use upgraded framing, improved moisture management, thicker drywall, and higher-grade materials throughout—not because they're required to, but because their reputation depends on every home they build.

And because local builders live and work in the communities they build in, they have a personal stake in getting it right.

Their name is on every house. They're answering to their neighbors, and that kind of accountability matters. In my experience, it shows in the quality of the finished product.

THE CASE FOR EXISTING HOMES

Existing homes often offer more space for the money you spend, especially in established neighborhoods where land was less expensive when the homes were originally built. You might get more square footage, a larger yard, or a better lot than you would with new construction at the same price point. Land costs account for a significant share of new-home prices, particularly in desirable areas.

Established neighborhoods have a known character. The trees are mature, providing shade and privacy that new developments won't have for years. The community has formed, and you can see what it's actually like. You can meet the neighbors, observe how the area is maintained, and see the traffic patterns and noise levels firsthand. With new construction in developing areas, you're projecting based on plans and promises—you don't always know what the neighborhood will become.

Existing homes are typically move-in ready. There's no construction timeline to navigate, no delays waiting for completion, and no hoping that your closing date aligns with when you need to be out of your current place. You close, you get keys, you move in. The process is more predictable and often faster.

Some buyers prefer the character and craftsmanship of older homes—the architectural details, the solid construction methods of earlier eras, the sense of history and permanence. Not every home needs to be new to be right.

UNDERSTANDING THE TRADE-OFFS

New construction typically costs more per square foot than comparable existing homes in the same general area. You're paying for new materials at current prices, current labor costs, modern features and efficiencies, and builder profit margins. If maximizing square footage per dollar is your primary goal, existing homes usually win that calculation.

But existing homes often need updates sooner. That kitchen that worked fine in 1995 might not meet your standards today. Bathrooms may need renovation. Flooring might need replacement. Systems—HVAC, water heater, roof—may be approaching the end of their useful lives. Factor in potential renovation and replacement costs into your comparison.

New-construction timelines can be unpredictable. Weather delays, labor shortages, material supply issues, and permitting complications—all can push completion dates further out than originally planned. If you need to coordinate the sale of your current home or end a lease, this uncertainty creates stress that existing home purchases typically avoid.

Location options differ significantly. New construction is typically in developing areas on the suburban edge, where land is available. If you want to be closer to urban centers, near specific schools, or in established neighborhoods with particular character, existing homes may be your only realistic option.

Inspections and due diligence also play out differently. With an existing home, a thorough home inspection is absolutely critical. You need to know the condition of the roof, the age and state of the HVAC system, the plumbing, the electrical, the foundation—everything. Surprises after closing on a resale home can be expensive. With new construction, you're dealing with brand-new systems and materials, and the builder's warranty provides a safety net. Many buyers still hire an independent inspector before closing on new construction, and I encourage it. A fresh set of eyes can catch things that were missed during the build, and a good builder will welcome the accountability.

Resale value and appreciation are worth considering as well. New construction in a growing area can appreciate quickly as the community develops, infrastructure improves, and demand increases. Existing homes in established neighborhoods tend to appreciate more steadily, supported by the location's desirability, mature landscaping, and proximity to schools and amenities. Both can be excellent investments—the trajectory just looks a little different.

One more thing to keep in mind is the long-term ownership costs. As I covered in Chapter 7, new-construction homes can save you real money in those early years through lower maintenance costs, lower insurance premiums, and better energy efficiency. Those savings add up over time and can offset the higher per-square-foot price. When you're comparing a new home to a resale home at a similar price, don't just look at the sticker—look at what each one is going to cost you to live in over the next five to ten years. That's where the real comparison happens.

MAKING YOUR DECISION

Think honestly about what matters most to you and your family.

If energy efficiency, modern features, warranty protection, customization, and being the first owner are high priorities—and you can be flexible on timeline and location—new construction deserves serious consideration.

If established neighborhoods, more space for the money, mature landscaping, known community character, and faster, more predictable timelines matter more, existing homes might be the better fit.

Consider your appetite for projects. Existing homes often need work—sometimes immediately, sometimes over time. Are you willing and able to handle renovations, updates, and ongoing maintenance of older systems? Or do you want move-in ready and minimal projects for the first several years?

Consider your timeline flexibility. Can you wait for construction, potentially dealing with and risking delays? Or do you need to be in a home by a specific date?

There's no universally right answer. I've helped families find happiness in both directions. The key is to be honest about your priorities and choose accordingly, rather than assuming one path is inherently better than the other.

• • • RESOURCE • • •

If you want to compare the numbers side by side, head over to www.justinskeytohomelife.com and use the free calculators in the Free Home-buying Tools section. You can run different scenarios for new construction versus resale, factor in maintenance costs, insurance estimates, and energy savings, and determine which option makes the most financial sense for your specific situation.

Whatever direction you choose, go in with your eyes open and your expectations set. Both paths lead to homeownership, and both can lead to a home your family loves for years to come.

•••JUSTIN'S TIP•••

With new construction, the model home is designed to sell you upgrades. That gorgeous kitchen? It probably has $40,000 in upgrades. Know the base price and get a full list of what's included versus what costs extra before you fall in love.

CHAPTER 11
Finding the Right Real Estate Professionals

• • •

The people who guide you through the home-buying process make an enormous difference in your experience and outcome. A great real estate professional makes the process smoother, catches problems early, negotiates effectively on your behalf, and often saves you money or headaches. A mediocre one adds friction, misses issues, and leaves value on the table.

Choosing the right people to work with is one of the most important decisions you'll make in this journey.

WHAT A BUYER'S AGENT DOES

A buyer's agent represents your interests in the home purchase transaction. They help you find properties that meet your criteria, arrange showings at times that work for your schedule, provide market knowledge and context, advise on pricing and offer strategy, coordinate inspections and other due diligence, negotiate on your behalf, and guide you through the paperwork and process all the way to closing.

A good buyer's agent is part advisor, part coordinator, part advocate. They know the local market intimately—what neighborhoods are trending up or down, what prices are reasonable, what issues commonly arise in different areas or property types. They've seen hundreds of transactions and can help you avoid mistakes that first-time buyers commonly make.

Now, there's an important change you need to know about regarding how buyer's agents get paid. In August 2024, a major legal settlement involving the National Association of Realtors (NAR) changed the way real estate commissions work. Under the old system, the seller typically paid both their own agent's commission and the buyer's agent's commission, so buyers rarely paid their agent directly. That's no longer the default.

Under the new rules, sellers are no longer required to pay the buyer's agent commission. Buyer's agent compensation can no longer be advertised on the Multiple Listing Service (MLS). And before a buyer's agent can even show you a home, you're now required to sign a written agreement that spells out exactly what services they'll provide and how much they'll be compensated. This is actually a good thing for transparency—you'll know exactly what you're paying for up front.

What this means practically is that you may need to negotiate your buyer's agent's compensation as part of your purchase. In many cases, you can still ask the seller to cover your agent's commission as a seller concession—and many sellers are willing to do so, especially in a competitive market where they want to attract as many buyers as possible. But it's no longer automatic, and it needs to be part of the conversation from the beginning.

Don't let this change scare you away from having professional representation. A good buyer's agent is worth every penny, and there are ways to structure the deal so the cost doesn't come out of your pocket. Just make sure you understand the terms before you sign anything.

FINDING THE RIGHT AGENT

Start with recommendations from people you trust—friends, family members, coworkers who have recently bought or sold in your target area. Personal referrals from satisfied clients are usually the best indicator of quality. Ask specifically what they liked about working with the agent and whether they'd use them again.

Interview at least two or three agents before choosing one. This isn't a commitment—it's due diligence. Ask how long they've been in the business, how many buyers they've helped in the past year, what neighborhoods they know best, how they prefer to communicate, how responsive they are, and whether they work full-time in real estate or do it on the side.

Pay attention to how they listen. A good agent asks questions to understand your specific needs, timeline, and concerns before launching into a pitch about their services. They should be curious about your situation, not just eager to start showing you houses.

Ask for references from recent buyer clients and actually call them. Ask about responsiveness, market knowledge, negotiation skills, how problems were handled, and whether they'd use the agent again without hesitation.

Chemistry matters. You'll be working closely with this person during one of the biggest financial decisions of your life. You need to feel comfortable asking questions, expressing concerns, and trusting their guidance. If something feels off in the initial conversations, it probably won't get better.

EXPERIENCE OVER CONVENIENCE

I need to say something here that might be uncomfortable, but needs to be said. Don't pick your real estate agent based on personal relationships alone. Your cousin who just got their license last month, your neighbor who does real estate on the side, the friend of a friend who's "really nice"—nice doesn't close houses. Experience does.

This is the biggest financial transaction most families will ever make. You want someone who has been through dozens or hundreds of transactions, who knows how to handle problems when they come up, who has relationships with lenders, inspectors, and title companies, and who can navigate the unexpected without panicking. A brand-new agent is still learning on the job, and you don't want your home purchase to be their classroom. There's a time and place for giving someone a chance. Buying your first home isn't it.

RED FLAGS TO WATCH FOR

Whether you're working with an agent, a lender, or any other professional in this process, there are warning signs that should make you pause.

Be cautious of anyone who pressures you to skip the home inspection. An inspection is your opportunity to understand exactly what you're buying, and anyone who discourages it isn't looking out for your best interests. Be wary of agents who push you toward the top of your budget on every property instead of helping you find the right home at a price you're comfortable with. Watch for professionals who are hard to reach, slow to return calls or emails, or who don't explain things in a way you can understand. If you feel like you're being rushed, talked down to, or pressured into decisions you're not ready to make, that's a problem.

A good professional educates you, communicates clearly, respects your timeline, and puts your interests ahead of their commission check. If you're not getting that, it's okay to find someone else. You don't owe anyone your business just because you started a conversation with them.

WORKING WITH NEW-CONSTRUCTION SALES TEAMS

If you're considering new construction, you'll interact with builder sales representatives. It's important to understand their role and how it differs from that of a buyer's agent.

Builder sales reps represent the builder, not you. Their job is to sell homes for the builder at prices and terms favorable to the builder. That doesn't make them adversaries—most genuinely want to help families find the right home and have a good experience—but their primary obligation is to their employer, not to you.

You can still bring your own buyer's agent to new-construction purchases. The builder may offer incentives for not using an outside agent, but having independent representation often provides value that exceeds those incentives. An experienced agent can help you evaluate pricing compared to the broader market, negotiate upgrades and concessions, review contracts for concerning terms, and advocate for your interests throughout the process.

Whether you bring your own agent or not, understand that the person across the desk in the sales office works for the builder. Be a savvy consumer. Do your research. Ask questions. Don't assume everything is negotiable—but don't assume nothing is, either.

Now, I want to give you my perspective from the other side of that desk, because I've been the person sitting there for a long time. As a new-construction sales manager, yes, I work for the builder. But the way I approach my job—and the way any good sales professional should—is that the home buyers come first. I walk them through every detail of the construction process, help them understand their options, explain what's included and what's an upgrade, and make sure they know exactly what they're getting before they sign anything. I stay with them from the first conversation through closing and beyond.

The best new-construction sales professionals aren't just trying to hit a number. They're building relationships. They want you to love your home, refer your friends and family, and come back when you're ready to move up. That only happens when the experience is honest, thorough, and genuinely focused on what's best for the buyer. When you're visiting model homes and sales offices, pay attention to how the sales team treats you. Are they listening to your needs, or are they just pushing what they have available? Are they transparent about timelines, costs, and expectations? Do they follow up and follow through? The good ones will stand out.

One important detail if you plan to use a buyer's agent with new construction is to bring them with you on your very first visit, or at the very least register them before you walk in. Most builders require the agent to be present or registered on the first visit to be recognized and paid their commission. If you visit a community on your own first and then try to bring your agent later, the builder may not honor the agent's involvement. This is a common mistake that can cost your agent their commission and potentially affect your working relationship. If you have an agent, let them know where you're planning to visit and coordinate beforehand.

BUILDING YOUR TEAM

Beyond your real estate agent, you'll work with several other professionals during the home-buying process.

Your lender is crucial—arguably the most important member of your team after your agent. This isn't just someone who processes paperwork. A good lender communicates proactively, returns your calls quickly, explains things in plain language, and keeps the entire transaction on track. They should be accessible when you have questions, patient when you need something explained twice, and experienced with the type of loan you're using. If you're going with an FHA loan, make sure your lender is familiar with FHA requirements. If you're using a VA loan, find a lender who specializes in VA financing. The nuances matter, and an inexperienced lender can create delays or problems that put your closing at risk. Clear communication between your agent and lender keeps everyone aligned on timelines and requirements, and that coordination is what makes the difference between a smooth closing and a stressful one.

A home inspector examines the property's condition before you finalize the purchase. Choose someone thorough, experienced, and independent—not necessarily whoever your agent casually suggests. You want an inspector who'll find problems and explain them clearly, not one who glosses over issues to keep deals moving.

A real estate attorney reviews contracts and handles the closing in some states. Even where attorneys aren't required, legal review of major contracts can catch issues that others miss. The cost is usually modest compared to the stakes involved.

An insurance agent helps you secure homeowner's coverage. Don't wait until the last minute—get quotes early from multiple carriers, and explore bundling with auto insurance for potential discounts.

A title company or escrow officer handles the closing process, ensuring that all documents are properly executed and funds are distributed correctly.

These professionals form your team. Choose each one carefully, communicate clearly with all of them, and remember that they work for you—you're the client.

COMMUNICATION IS EVERYTHING

The one thing that ties all of this together is communication. The best team in the world won't help you if nobody is talking to each other. Your agent must maintain regular contact with your lender. Your lender needs to communicate with the title company. If you're buying new construction, your sales manager needs to keep your lender updated on the build timeline. And you need to be responsive when any of these people reach out to you.

I've seen deals fall apart not because of money or credit, or the property itself, but because someone dropped the ball on communication. A document required by Tuesday wasn't sent until Friday. A phone call that should have taken five minutes went unanswered. An email with important instructions sat unread for a week. Don't let that be you. When your team asks for something, get it to them quickly. When they call, call back. When they email, respond. The faster everyone communicates, the smoother the process goes.

Buying a home is a team effort. Surround yourself with experienced, trustworthy professionals who genuinely care about getting you into the right home at the right price. Set clear expectations about communication from the start. And don't be afraid to ask questions—there are no dumb questions when you're making the biggest purchase of your life—the right team will welcome every single one.

•••KEY TAKEAWAY•••

The rules have changed. As of 2024, you sign a buyer agency agreement before touring homes with an agent. This agreement specifies how your agent will be compensated. Don't be afraid to ask questions and negotiate. Understand what you're agreeing to.

CHAPTER 12

The Art of the Home Search

• • •

This is the fun part. Walking through homes and imagining your life in them. Envisioning your furniture in those rooms and picturing your kids playing in that backyard. Seeing yourself cooking in that kitchen, relaxing in that living room, waking up in that bedroom.

But the home search is also where emotions can override good judgment. Where you can fall in love with the wrong house, overlook serious problems because of cosmetic appeal, or miss the right opportunity while waiting for something perfect that doesn't exist. A strategic approach helps you find a home you'll love for years without making costly mistakes.

DEFINING YOUR CRITERIA

Before you look at a single property, get crystal clear on what you're looking for. This sounds obvious, but many buyers skip this step and end up confused, overwhelmed, or making decisions they later regret.

Start with your needs—the absolute non-negotiables. Maybe it's a minimum number of bedrooms for your family size. A specific school district for your children. Proximity to work within a certain commute time. A garage for your vehicle. Whatever you absolutely, definitely require, write it down. These are your filters—properties that don't meet them get rejected, period.

Then list your wants—features you'd love to have but could live without if everything else is right. A separate dining room. A particular architectural style. A swimming pool. Extra garage space. A home office. A large yard. These are your preferences—nice-to-haves, not dealbreakers.

Be ruthlessly honest about the difference between needs and wants. If you confuse them, you'll either reject good options over minor preferences or accept poor options because exciting features distracted you from missing essentials.

Discuss and align on this list with anyone who'll be living in the home. If you and your spouse or partner have different ideas about what's essential, work that out before you start touring properties. Discovering fundamental disagreements while standing in someone's living room leads to arguments and bad decisions.

RESEARCHING NEIGHBORHOODS

You're not just buying a house—you're buying into a neighborhood, a community, a location. You can change almost anything about a house over time, but you can't change where it sits.

Drive through potential neighborhoods at different times of day and different days of the week. Morning rush hour reveals traffic patterns and commute realities. Evening and weekend visits reveal how neighbors use their properties, what noise levels are like, and general activity. You'll see different things at different times.

Check crime statistics for areas you're considering. Research school ratings and boundaries if you have or plan to have children. Look up sex offender registries. Investigate flood zones, wildfire risk, and other natural disaster histories relevant to your region.

Talk to people who live there if you can. Neighbors are often willing to share their honest opinions about the area—what they love, what frustrates them, what's changed recently. Local business owners can also offer a useful perspective.

Consider future development. Are there vacant lots nearby that might become something you don't want next door? Any commercial development in the planning stages? Major road projects that could change traffic patterns or noise levels? These factors can dramatically alter a location's character.

THE ONLINE SEARCH

Most home searches today start online, and there's nothing wrong with that. Sites like Zillow, Realtor.com, and Redfin give you access to listings, photos, price histories, and neighborhood data from your couch. Builder websites show you floor plans, virtual tours, and community information. Use all of these tools—they're a great starting point.

But understand their limitations. Photos can be misleading—wide-angle lenses make rooms look bigger than they are, professional lighting flatters every surface, and you can't smell a musty basement or hear highway noise from a photo. Don't eliminate a home based on photos alone, and don't fall in love based on photos alone. The only way to really know a home is to walk through it and experience the space, the neighborhood, and the feel of being there in person.

SEARCHING FOR NEW CONSTRUCTION

If you're considering new construction, the search process looks a little different. You're not touring someone's lived-in home—you're walking through model homes, reading site plans, and choosing from available lots and floor plans. It's a different experience, and there are a few things to keep in mind.

Model homes are designed to sell. They're typically loaded with upgrades, professionally decorated, and staged to showcase each room at its best. That's fine—just understand the difference between the model and the base home you're actually pricing. Always ask for the base price and a clear breakdown of what's included versus what's an upgrade. The beautiful kitchen you're admiring in the model might cost significantly more than the standard one.

Pay attention to the site plan. Lot selection matters—the same floor plan can feel completely different depending on whether it backs to trees, faces another home, or sits on a corner. Ask about future phases of the community. What's being built next to you? What will the view look like in two years? A good sales team will be transparent about all of this. And take your time. With new construction, you have the advantage of thinking through your decisions, customizing your selections with some builders—not all offer this level of personalization—and building something that truly fits your family. Don't rush it.

MANAGING THE SEARCH PROCESS

Set up automated alerts for new listings matching your criteria. In competitive markets, desirable properties can get under contract within hours or days of listing. Being among the first to know about new listings gives you an advantage.

Keep organized records of what you see. After touring ten or fifteen homes, they start to blur together. Take photos and notes at each property, even if they're brief ones. Record what you liked, what you didn't, any concerns or questions that arose. This documentation helps when you're comparing options or recalling details later.

Stay focused on your established criteria. It's easy to be distracted by beautiful staging, by one amazing feature, by the excitement of the search itself. Keep returning to your list of needs and wants. Does this property actually meet your requirements? Or are you being seduced by things that don't ultimately matter?

Permit yourself to walk away quickly from properties that clearly don't work. You don't need to examine every room of every house. If the neighborhood is wrong, if the layout fundamentally doesn't fit your life, if essential requirements aren't met—move on. Save your time and energy for properties that have real potential.

THE EMOTIONAL ROLLERCOASTER

I want to prepare you for what almost every buyer goes through—an emotional rollercoaster of a home search. You'll find homes you love that get under contract before you can make an offer. You'll lose out on offers to other buyers who came in higher or faster. You'll feel frustrated, discouraged, and maybe even a little panicked that you'll never find the right one.

This is normal. It happens to almost everyone. And the worst thing you can do is panic-buy out of fear that you're going to miss out. Buying the wrong home out of fear of losing another is far worse than waiting patiently for the right opportunity. I tell the families I work with this all the time that the right home will come. Trust the process, stay disciplined with your criteria and your budget, and don't let fear make a decision that should be made with clarity.

SEEING PAST THE SURFACE

Staging and cosmetic touches can dramatically affect how a home feels during a showing. That's exactly why sellers use them. Your job is to see past the surface to the bones underneath.

Ignore paint colors—paint is cheap and easy to change. Ignore most furniture and décor—it's leaving with the current owners anyway. Focus on things that are expensive or impossible to change: layout, lot position, natural light, ceiling heights, and structural elements.

Look for signs of deferred maintenance or problems being covered up. Fresh paint in one room but not others may indicate water damage or other hidden issues. Notice musty smells, ceiling stains, and cracks in walls or foundations. These could be minor or red flags for larger problems.

Consider the flow of daily life. Where would you put your furniture? How would morning routines work with this bathroom configuration? Where would kids do homework? Where would you unwind at the end of the day? Visualize your actual life in the space, not just a generic idea of what it would be like to live there.

WHEN YOU FIND THE ONE

You'll know when a property clicks. It meets your essential criteria. It feels right. You can see your life there in a way that previous properties didn't quite achieve.

When that happens, be prepared to act. Have your preapproval letter ready. Know what you can reasonably offer. Be in close communication with your agent.

But don't let excitement override good judgment. The home still needs inspection. The price still needs to make sense for the market and your budget. Your offer should be competitive but not reckless. The right home at the wrong price is the wrong home. Stay grounded even when emotions are running high.

ALWAYS GO BACK A SECOND TIME

Before you make an offer on any resale home, go back for a second visit. If you can, schedule a different time of day than your first showing. A house that felt quiet and peaceful on a Tuesday afternoon might back up to a busy road that's packed during Friday rush hour. A neighborhood that seemed calm during the day might be noisy on a weekend evening.

Bring someone with fresh eyes if you can—a parent, a trusted friend, someone who isn't emotionally invested. They'll notice things you missed because you were too excited the first time. The second visit is where you shift from "I love this house" to "Does this house actually work for my life?" That's an important distinction.

THINK ABOUT RESALE VALUE

Even if you think this is your forever home, think about resale value. Life is unpredictable—job changes, family changes, financial changes—and you may need or want to sell sooner than you planned. When that day comes, you want a home that other buyers will want too.

Avoid being the most expensive home on the block—the less expensive homes around you will drag your value down instead of improving it. Be cautious about corner lots on busy intersections, homes that back onto commercial property, houses directly under power lines, or properties on roads with heavy traffic. These details don't bother some buyers, but they narrow your pool of future buyers significantly, and that affects what you can sell for down the road. A home is both a place to live and an investment. Keep both in mind during your search.

WHAT I TELL MY FAMILIES

After nearly thirty years of helping families find homes, I've seen every mistake in the book. I've seen buyers fall in love with a home for its beautiful kitchen and completely overlook a failing foundation. I've seen families buy the first house they toured because they were too excited to keep looking. I've seen people stretch way past their budget because they got caught up in the moment and talked themselves into payments they couldn't comfortably afford.

Here's what I tell every family I work with. Take your time. Be patient. Stay within your budget. Don't let anyone rush you. And remember that no home is perfect. You're looking for the home that checks the most important boxes for your family at a price that lets you sleep at night. When you find that, you've found the one. Everything else can be improved over time. That's the beauty of homeownership—it's yours to shape into exactly what you want.

•••JUSTIN'S TIP•••

You're not going to find a perfect house. You'll find a house that checks most of your boxes and feels right. The families I've seen happiest are the ones who knew which boxes truly mattered and let go of the rest.

CHAPTER 13

FROM OFFER TO CONTRACT

• • •

YOU'VE FOUND A HOME you love. It meets your criteria, fits within your budget, and feels right for your family. Now comes one of the most nerve-wracking parts of the entire process: making an offer and negotiating a contract.

This is where many buyers feel completely out of their depth. The stakes are high, the process is unfamiliar, and there's pressure to make quick decisions without much time to think. Understanding how it all works helps you navigate with confidence.

CRAFTING YOUR OFFER

An offer to purchase includes several key elements beyond just the price you're willing to pay.

The offered price is obviously central to any offer. Your agent should provide comparable sales data—what similar properties in the area have actually sold for recently—to help you determine a reasonable offer. In balanced markets, starting somewhat below the asking price and negotiating toward the middle is common. In hot markets with multiple competing buyers, you may need to offer at or above the asking price to remain competitive.

Earnest money demonstrates your serious intent to purchase. This deposit—typically 1 to 3 percent of the purchase price—goes into an escrow account when your offer is accepted. It's applied toward your down payment at closing. If you back out of the deal for reasons not covered by your contingencies, you may forfeit some or all of it.

Proposed closing date and possession date matter to sellers, sometimes as much as price. Flexibility here can make a lower offer more attractive than a higher one that's rigid on timing. Understand the seller's needs and, if you can, accommodate them.

Contingencies protect you by allowing you to back out of the contract under specified circumstances without losing your earnest money. Common contingencies include financing (if your loan falls through despite good-faith efforts), inspection (if the inspection reveals significant problems), and appraisal (if the home doesn't appraise at the agreed purchase price).

ESCALATION CLAUSES

In competitive markets where multiple offers are common, some buyers include an escalation clause in their offer. An escalation clause automatically increases your offer by a set amount above any competing offer, up to a maximum cap that you define. For example, you might offer $350,000 with an escalation clause that says you'll beat any competing offer by $2,000 up to a maximum of $370,000. If another buyer offers $360,000, your offer will automatically increase to $362,000.

Escalation clauses can be effective, but they come with trade-offs. The upside is you stay competitive without unthinkingly overbidding. The downside is that you're revealing your maximum price to the seller, which weakens your negotiating position. Some sellers and listing agents don't accept escalation clauses at all. Talk to your agent about whether one makes sense for your specific situation and market conditions.

SELLER CONCESSIONS

A seller concession is when the seller agrees to contribute money toward your closing costs or other expenses as part of the deal. This can be a powerful tool, especially for first-time buyers who have enough for a down payment but are stretched thin on closing costs.

With the recent changes in how buyer's agent commissions work—which I covered in Chapter 11—seller concessions have become even more relevant. You can now ask the seller to contribute toward your buyer's agent commission as part of the concession, in addition to closing costs. How you structure this depends on your loan type, as each program has limits on seller contributions. FHA loans typically allow up to 6 percent of the purchase price in seller concessions, while conventional loans allow 3 to 9 percent, depending on your down payment. VA loans have their own guidelines. Your lender and agent can help you figure out what's possible and how to structure it in your offer.

THE HOME SALE CONTINGENCY

If you need to sell your current home to buy the new one, you may need to include a home sale contingency in your offer. This makes your purchase conditional on selling your existing property first. It's understandable—most people can't carry two mortgages at once—but you need to know that this contingency significantly weakens your offer in the eyes of most sellers.

A seller accepting a home sale contingency is essentially agreeing to take their home off the market and wait for you to sell yours, with no guarantee that it will happen on time—or at all. In a competitive market, sellers with multiple offers will almost always choose a buyer without this contingency. If you're in this situation, talk to your agent and lender about alternatives. A bridge loan, a home equity line of credit, or timing the sale of your current home before you start making offers can all strengthen your position. The stronger and cleaner your offer, the better your chances of getting the home you want.

UNDERSTANDING CONTINGENCIES

Contingencies are your protection, and understanding them is crucial.

A financing contingency protects you if your mortgage approval falls through. If you've done everything required but the lender still denies your loan, you can exit the contract and get your earnest money back.

An inspection contingency gives you the right to have the property professionally inspected and to negotiate repairs, credits, or a withdrawal based on the inspection findings. This is critical protection—never waive inspection contingency unless you're extremely experienced and prepared to accept whatever unknown problems exist.

An appraisal contingency protects you if the home appraises below your agreed purchase price. Your lender won't lend more than appraised value, so without this contingency, you'd have to cover any gap with additional cash or risk losing your earnest money.

In highly competitive markets, buyers sometimes waive contingencies to make their offers more attractive to sellers. This is risky. Waiving inspection means accepting the property as-is, including problems you don't yet know about. Waiving appraisal means committing to cover any gap between the agreed price and the appraised value out of pocket. Think very carefully before giving up these protections.

NEGOTIATING EFFECTIVELY

Most offers lead to counteroffers. The seller might counter on price, closing date, contingency terms, or other elements. Then you can accept their counteroffer, reject it and walk away, or counter with your own. This back-and-forth continues until both parties agree or someone walks away.

Understand what matters most to each party. For some sellers, speed and certainty matter more than getting every last dollar. For others, the highest price is everything. For others, a flexible closing date that aligns with their purchase timeline is the priority. Your agent can often gather intelligence on seller motivations, helping you craft more effective offers.

Don't negotiate over trivial amounts when you've found the right home. Getting stuck on minor points and losing the deal over a few hundred dollars is penny-wise and pound-foolish. Know what matters and what doesn't.

But also know your limits. If negotiations push the price or terms beyond what makes sense for your situation, be prepared to walk away. There will be other houses. Never let emotional attachment cause you to overextend or accept terms that put you at risk.

MULTIPLE OFFER SITUATIONS

In a competitive market, you may find yourself in a multiple offer situation where several buyers are bidding on the same property. When this happens, the seller's agent will typically notify all interested parties that multiple offers have been received and may ask for "best and final" offers by a specific deadline.

Price matters in these situations, but it's not the only factor sellers consider. A strong preapproval letter from a reputable lender signals that your financing is solid and unlikely to fall through. Clean contingencies—or fewer of them—reduce the seller's risk. Flexibility on the closing date and possession shows you're easy to work with. A larger earnest money deposit demonstrates serious commitment. Some buyers even include a personal letter to the seller explaining why they love the home and what it would mean to their family. Not every seller cares about that, but some do, and it can make a difference when two offers are otherwise close.

The most important part of a multiple offer situation is to submit the strongest offer you're comfortable with the first time. Don't hold back thinking you'll get a chance to negotiate—you may not. Put your best foot forward and then accept whatever happens. If you win it, great. If you don't, the right home is still out there.

WHAT I'VE SEEN GO WRONG

I've been on both sides of this process for nearly thirty years, and I've seen the offer and negotiation phase go sideways in completely avoidable ways. I've seen buyers lose homes they loved because they tried to lowball in a hot market, only for the seller not even to bother to counter. I've seen buyers waive their inspection contingency to win a bidding war, only to end up with tens of thousands of dollars in repairs they didn't know about. I've seen deals fall apart the week before closing because someone opened a new credit card to buy furniture.

The offer and negotiation process is stressful. I won't sugarcoat that. But it doesn't have to be chaotic. Trust your agent's advice—this is where their experience matters most. Stay calm, stay rational, and keep your eyes on the big picture. You're not just winning a negotiation. You're making one of the biggest financial commitments of your life. Treat it that way, lean on the professionals around you, and you'll come out the other side in great shape.

UNDER CONTRACT

When buyer and seller agree on all terms, you're officially under contract. This is a significant milestone—but it's not the finish line.

Now the due diligence period begins. Inspections need to happen. The appraisal needs to be completed. Your lender needs to finalize your loan approval. Title search must confirm clear ownership. All of this takes time and coordination, and things can still go wrong.

Stay in close communication with your agent and lender throughout this period. Respond promptly to any requests for documentation or decisions. Meet all deadlines specified in the contract—missing deadlines can have serious consequences, including losing your earnest money or the deal itself.

And remember our earlier warning. Don't do anything to jeopardize your financing during this period: no new credit accounts, no large purchases, and no job changes. Keep your financial life stable and boring until you have keys in hand.

The period between going under contract and closing can feel like it's taking forever. There's a lot of hurry-up-and-wait—where you'll submit documents, answer questions, schedule inspections, and then sit and wait for other people to do their part. This is normal. Resist the urge to call your agent or lender daily for updates. Trust that they're working the process. If something needs your attention, they'll reach out.

That said, if you haven't heard anything in a while and your closing date is approaching, a polite check-in is perfectly fine. You have every right to know where things stand. Just remember that everyone on your team—your agent, your lender, the title company, the other side's agent—is typically managing multiple transactions at once. A little patience goes a long way, and so does being the buyer who responds quickly and has their documents ready when asked. The smoother you make it for your team, the smoother they'll make it for you.

• • • WATCH OUT • • •

Never waive the inspection contingency to win a bidding war. I've seen buyers win the house but inherit $30,000 in problems they didn't know about. A home inspection is a few hundred dollars that can save you tens of thousands. It's not worth the risk.

CHAPTER 14

Inspections, Appraisals, and Closing Day

• • •

Your offer was accepted. You're officially under contract. But the period between signing the contract and receiving the keys is when the real due diligence occurs. Inspections reveal the property's true condition. The appraisal confirms the home's value. Your lender completes final underwriting. And then, if everything checks out, you close.

This period is exciting but also anxiety-inducing. Things can go wrong. Problems can surface. Deals can fall apart. Understanding the process helps you navigate it successfully.

THE HOME INSPECTION

A professional home inspection is a comprehensive examination of the property's condition, and it's one of the most important steps in your due diligence. Never skip it, even if you're buying new construction.

The inspector will examine the roof, foundation, structural elements, exterior surfaces, electrical system, plumbing, HVAC, water heater, insulation, ventilation, appliances, and more. They'll identify existing problems, potential safety hazards, deferred maintenance, and items that may need attention in the near future.

Attend the inspection if you possibly can. Walking through with the inspector, seeing issues firsthand, and asking questions teaches you things about the home you're buying that no written report can fully convey. You should budget three to four hours for a typical inspection.

Every home inspection finds issues. Don't panic when problems surface. Some issues are minor maintenance items common to any home. Others are more significant but expected for the home's age and type. The question isn't whether there are issues—there always are—it's whether the issues are dealbreakers, negotiation points, or simply things to be aware of as you become the owner.

Focus on the big stuff: structural integrity, roof condition, foundation soundness, and major systems such as electrical, plumbing, and HVAC. Cosmetic issues and minor repairs matter less—you can address those over time once you own the home.

Based on inspection findings, you typically have options under your contract terms: accept the property as-is, request repairs, request credits toward closing costs, renegotiate the purchase price, or exercise your inspection contingency to withdraw from the deal. Your agent can advise on what's reasonable to request given market conditions and the nature of issues found.

SPECIALIZED INSPECTIONS

A general home inspection covers a lot of ground, but it doesn't cover everything. Depending on the property, area, and the house's age, you may want or need specialized inspections beyond the standard one.

Radon testing is important in many parts of the country. Radon is a naturally occurring radioactive gas that can seep into homes through the foundation, and long-term exposure is a serious health concern. Testing is inexpensive, and mitigation is straightforward if levels are elevated, but you need to know before you buy.

Termite and pest inspections check for wood-destroying insects and other organisms that can cause significant structural damage—in many areas, lenders require this inspection.

A sewer scope sends a camera through the sewer line to check for cracks, root intrusion, bellies, or deterioration. Replacing a sewer line can cost thousands of dollars, and this is one of those problems that a general inspection won't catch.

If the home has a well and septic system instead of public water and sewer, those need to be tested separately. Well water should be tested for quality and flow rate. The septic system should be inspected and pumped to confirm proper operation.

Mold testing may be warranted if you notice signs of water damage or smell musty odors.

Your agent and inspector can help you determine which specialized inspections make sense for the specific property you're buying. The cost of these additional tests is minimal compared to the cost of discovering a major problem after closing.

THE APPRAISAL

Your lender requires an appraisal to confirm that the home's market value supports the loan amount. They're lending hundreds of thousands of dollars with the property as collateral—they want to make sure that collateral is worth what you're paying.

An independent, licensed appraiser will visit the property, assess its condition and features, research recent comparable sales in the area, and determine its market value. This isn't based on what you agreed to pay—it's based on what the evidence suggests the home is actually worth.

If the appraisal comes in at or above the purchase price, great—you proceed as usual. The lender is satisfied that the collateral supports the loan.

If the appraisal comes in low—below your agreed purchase price—you have several options. You can renegotiate with the seller to reduce the purchase price to the appraised value. You can pay the difference between the appraised value and the purchase price in additional cash (the appraisal gap). You can challenge the appraisal with evidence of comparable sales that the appraiser may have missed. Or you can exercise your appraisal contingency to withdraw from the contract.

Low appraisals aren't common in most markets. But they do happen, especially in rapidly appreciating markets where sales prices outpace comparable data, or for unique properties where good comparables are hard to find. Having an appraisal contingency protects you from being forced to overpay or lose your earnest money.

FINAL LOAN APPROVAL

Your preapproval was conditional. Now your lender completes final underwriting based on the specific property you're purchasing.

They'll verify that nothing in your financial situation has changed since preapproval—same job, same income, no new debts, no large unexplained deposits. They'll review the appraisal to confirm the property supports the loan. They'll review the title search to confirm ownership is clear. They'll confirm homeowner's insurance is in place. They'll check and clear dozens of conditions.

Stay responsive during this period. If your lender requests additional documentation, provide it immediately. Answer any questions promptly and completely. Delays in your responses delay your closing.

Once all conditions are satisfied, you receive "clear to close"—official confirmation that your loan is fully approved and you're ready to proceed to closing.

THE FINAL WALK THROUGH

Shortly before closing—usually within twenty-four to forty-eight hours—you'll do a final walk through of the property. This isn't another inspection. This is your chance to verify that the home is in the condition you expect before you take ownership.

Confirm that any repairs the seller agreed to make have actually been completed. Make sure nothing has been damaged since your last visit—moving furniture out of a home sometimes reveals wall damage, floor scratches, or holes that weren't visible before. Verify that all fixtures, appliances, and items included in the contract are still in place. Run the faucets, flush the toilets, flip the light switches, and test the HVAC. Open and close doors and windows. Check the garage door. Look at the yard.

If you discover any problems during the walk through, raise them immediately with your agent before you go to the closing table. It's much easier to address issues before you've signed everything than after. Don't skip the walk through because you're busy or because everything seemed fine at the inspection. Things change, and this is your last chance to catch them.

WIRE FRAUD WARNING

I need to discuss one of the most serious threats in real estate today: wire fraud. This isn't hypothetical. People lose their entire down payment to this scam every year, and once the money is gone, it's rarely recovered.

Here's how it works. Scammers hack into email accounts—yours, your agent's, the title company's, or your lender's—and monitor the transaction. Right before closing, they send you an email that appears to be from the title company or closing attorney, complete with logos and official-looking formatting. The email contains wiring instructions for your closing funds. You then wire the money, but the account belongs to the scammer, not the title company. And just like that, your life savings are gone.

Protect yourself. Always verify wiring instructions by phone before you send a single dollar—and use a phone number you already have on file with the title company, not one from the email. Never trust wiring instructions that arrive by email alone, even if they look legitimate. If the instructions change at the last minute, that's a massive red flag. Call your title company directly and confirm before you do anything. This is one of those warnings that feels like it could never happen to you until it does. Take it seriously.

CLOSING DAY

Closing day is when ownership officially transfers from the seller to you. You'll sign a substantial stack of documents, provide your remaining funds, and—finally—receive the keys to your new home.

Before closing, carefully review your "closing disclosure," which details all final loan terms, monthly payment breakdown, and itemized closing costs. Lenders are required to provide this at least three business days before closing, giving you time to review it and ask questions about any unexpected items.

Compare your closing disclosure to your original "loan estimate." Some variation is normal and permitted, but significant unexpected increases should be questioned and explained.

Bring valid government-issued identification to closing, typically a driver's license or passport. Bring your funds as directed by the closing agent—this is usually a wire transfer or cashier's check for the exact amount specified. Personal checks are generally not accepted for closing funds.

The closing itself involves signing numerous documents: the promissory note (your promise to repay the loan), the mortgage or deed of trust (which gives the lender a security interest in the property), various disclosures, and the deed transferring ownership. A closing agent or attorney will guide you through each document and answer questions.

And then, after all the preparation and searching and negotiating and waiting, someone hands you keys. You're a homeowner.

Take a breath. You did it. Welcome to homeownership.

Plan for the closing to take about an hour, though it may be slightly longer. Depending on your state, you may be sitting at a table with your agent, the seller and their agent, the closing attorney or title officer, and possibly your lender's representative. In some cases, the buyer and seller close separately or at different times. Your agent or closing attorney will let you know what to expect for your specific situation. Don't be afraid to ask questions during closing—you should understand everything you're signing. If something doesn't look right or doesn't match what you were told, speak up before you sign it.

THE MOMENT IT ALL BECOMES REAL

I've been part of more closings than I can count, and the moment someone gets handed those keys never gets old. I've seen tears. I've seen families hug each other in the parking lot. I've seen first-time buyers sit in their car afterward just staring at the keys in their hand, trying to process that they actually did it.

That feeling is real, and you'll have earned it. Everything you went through to get there—the saving, the stress, the paperwork, the waiting, the uncertainty—it all leads to this moment. My advice on closing day is simple. Enjoy it. Take a photo with your keys. Drive to your new house and walk through every room, this time knowing it's yours. Let it sink in. You worked hard for this, and you deserve to feel every bit of it.

• • •

CLOSING DAY CHECKLIST

• • •

- ☐ Review closing disclosure (received at least three days before)
- ☐ Confirm wire transfer instructions directly with the title company
- ☐ Obtain a cashier's check or schedule a wire transfer
- ☐ Complete final walk through of the property
- ☐ Bring government-issued photo ID
- ☐ Bring proof of homeowners insurance
- ☐ Review all documents before signing
- ☐ Receive the keys!

• • • WATCH OUT • • •

Wire fraud is real and devastating. Criminals hack email accounts and send fake wire instructions. *Always* call the title company directly using a number you looked up yourself—not one from an email—to verify wire instructions. One wrong click can cost you your entire down payment.

PART THREE
MAKING IT YOURS

CHAPTERS 15–20

A HOUSE BECOMES A HOME WHEN YOU MAKE IT REFLECT WHO YOU ARE.

CHAPTER 15

Design Principles That Transform Spaces

• • •

Your house is a building. Your home is what you create inside it. The difference between a house that merely shelters you and a home that truly serves and delights you comes down to thoughtful design choices.

Good design isn't about following trends or spending a fortune. It's about understanding how spaces work and making choices that serve how you actually live. The most beautifully decorated room that doesn't function for your daily life isn't good design—it's just expensive decoration.

I'm not a professional interior designer, but I've worked alongside them throughout my career, and I've watched hundreds of families settle into new homes over the years. I've seen what works and what doesn't. I've observed which choices bring lasting satisfaction and which ones people quickly regret. And I've learned that the happiest homeowners aren't necessarily those with the biggest budgets—they're the ones who understand a few fundamental principles.

START BY LIVING IN IT

The biggest mistake new homeowners make is rushing to decorate and furnish immediately. They move in, and the very first weekend they're out buying furniture, hanging things on walls, and making permanent decisions about spaces they barely understand yet.

Don't do this. Live in the space first. Take at least three months, ideally six, before making major design decisions or significant purchases.

During this time, pay attention. Notice how natural light moves through the rooms at different times of day and different seasons. See which areas you naturally gravitate toward and which ones you rarely use. Discover where traffic flows smoothly and where bottlenecks form. Learn where sound carries and where quiet spaces exist. Identify which storage you need and where you wish you had more.

This lived experience is invaluable. It prevents costly mistakes such as buying a sectional that blocks the natural flow of a room, renovating a space that didn't actually need changing while ignoring one that did, or hanging art on a wall that turns out to be the only logical place for the TV.

Patience pays off. The home will tell you what it needs if you give it time to speak.

FLOW AND FUNCTION FIRST

Good design supports how you actually live, not how you think you should live or how magazine photos suggest you should live.

Think about how your family moves through the home on a typical day. From the garage to the kitchen with arms full of groceries. From the bedroom to the bathroom during the morning rush. From the living area to the backyard, where kids can burn energy. From the home office to the kitchen for coffee breaks. These pathways should be clear and logical, not obstructed by furniture placement or awkward layouts.

Think about where you actually spend time versus where you think you should spend time. Many families have formal living rooms that remain empty while everyone crams into a small den. Many have dining rooms used twice a year for holidays, while everyday meals happen at kitchen counters or in front of the TV. Let reality guide your design choices rather than traditional expectations.

Consider which activities need a dedicated space. Working from home requires different considerations than a purely recreational space. Kids doing homework need surfaces and lighting. Hobbies that spread out—crafts, puzzles, projects—need areas where they can remain in progress. Exercise equipment must be accessible for actual use. Create zones that support your actual daily life.

THE POWER OF LIGHT

Light affects how a room feels more than almost any other single factor. Dark rooms feel cramped, dreary, and sometimes even depressing. Light-filled rooms feel open, welcoming, and energizing.

Before you think about paint colors, before you buy furniture, before you hang anything on walls—consider light. How can you maximize it? Can you strategically add mirrors to reflect natural light deeper into the rooms? Can window treatments be adjusted to let in more light while still maintaining privacy? Are there areas where additional lighting fixtures would transform the space?

Layer your lighting for flexibility. Ambient light—overhead fixtures, recessed cans—provides general illumination for a room. Task lighting—desk lamps, under-cabinet lights, reading lamps—focuses light on the area where specific activities occur. Accent lighting—picture lights, uplights, candles—highlights features and creates a mood. Most rooms benefit from having all three types available at different times.

Consider the color temperature of your bulbs. Warm light (2,700 to 3,000K) creates cozy, relaxing atmospheres suitable for living spaces and bedrooms. Cooler light (3,500 to 4,000K) is better suited for task-oriented spaces such as kitchens, bathrooms, and home offices. Mismatched color temperatures in the same room look odd and feel unsettling.

COLOR CHOICES THAT WORK

Paint is the single most impactful and least expensive change you can make to any room. The right color can make a small room feel larger, a cold room feel warmer, and a boring room feel alive. The wrong color can have the opposite effect.

Light colors—whites, soft grays, pale blues—open rooms up and reflect natural light, making spaces feel airy and spacious. They're safe choices that work almost everywhere. Darker colors can add warmth, drama, and sophistication in the right spaces—a deep navy accent wall in a bedroom, a rich green in a study—but they absorb light and can make small rooms feel smaller if you're not careful. An accent wall is a great way to introduce bold color without committing to it on every surface.

Here's the most important advice I can give about paint. Never pick a color from a tiny swatch and commit to an entire room. Buy sample pots and paint large swatches directly on the wall—at least two feet by two feet—in different spots around the room. Look at them in morning, afternoon, and evening light, with your artificial lighting on. Colors look completely different depending on the light, and what looked perfect at the store can look completely wrong on your wall. A few dollars in samples saves you the headache and expense of repainting.

THE ART OF EDITING

Sometimes the best design decision is to remove something rather than add to it. Clutter creates visual noise that makes spaces feel chaotic, small, and stressful—even in objectively large spaces.

You don't need to display every possession you own. You don't need to fill every surface with decorative objects. You don't need something on every wall. Empty space has value—it gives the eye places to rest and makes the things you do display more impactful.

Before buying anything new for your home, consider whether something existing could go. Trade the old for the new rather than simply accumulating more. Your home will feel larger, calmer, and more intentional.

This is particularly important when moving from a smaller space to a larger one. The furniture and belongings that filled your apartment may look sparse and insufficient in a house. The temptation is to buy more to fill the space. Resist that, at least initially. Live with the openness for a while. You might discover you prefer it. And you'll make better choices about what to add when you're not rushing to fill every corner.

ROOMS THAT DO DOUBLE DUTY

Most families don't have the luxury of dedicating every room to a single purpose. Real life requires flexibility. The guest room that sits empty eleven months a year can also be your home office. The dining room can double as homework central during the school week. A finished basement can serve as a playroom, a movie room, and an exercise space depending on the time of day.

The key to making multi-purpose rooms work is smart furniture choices and good organization. A desk with storage that can be closed when guests visit. A dining table that clears easily for homework or projects. Shelving that keeps supplies accessible but tidy. Consider how each room can serve your family in multiple ways, and design accordingly. You'll get far more value out of your square footage when every room earns its keep.

BUDGET-FRIENDLY CHANGES THAT MAKE A BIG IMPACT

You don't need a big budget to transform how your home looks and feels. Some of the most impactful changes cost almost nothing compared to major renovations.

Paint, as I mentioned, is the least expensive transformation option. A single weekend and a few gallons of paint can completely change a room's character. Swapping out cabinet hardware in a kitchen or bathroom—replacing dated brass knobs with modern brushed-nickel or matte-black pulls—takes an hour and costs under $100, but it updates the entire look. Replacing builder-grade light fixtures with fixtures that have more character can transform a room from generic to personal. New switch plates and outlet covers with a consistent finish throughout the home are small details that make everything feel more polished and intentional.

Focus your money on changes you'll see and touch every day. A beautiful faucet you use a dozen times a day brings more daily satisfaction than an expensive piece of art in a hallway you walk past without noticing. Prioritize the spaces where you spend the most time and the details you interact with the most.

CURB APPEAL AND FIRST IMPRESSIONS

Don't forget your house's exterior. How your home looks from the street affects how you feel every time you pull into the driveway, and it has a real impact on resale value over time.

A freshly painted front door is one of the simplest and most effective curb appeal upgrades. It's the focal point of your home's facade, and a bold color that complements your exterior can make the whole house look sharper. Clean landscaping—trimmed shrubs, fresh mulch, a few seasonal flowers—signals that someone cares about this property. Updated exterior lighting makes your home feel welcoming at night and improves security. Even small details, such as new house numbers and a clean mailbox, contribute to the overall impression. Stand at the curb, look at your home the way a visitor or a future buyer would, and ask yourself what could be better. Usually, a weekend of work and a modest investment can make a noticeable difference.

EVOLVING OVER TIME

Your home doesn't need to be finished the day you move in. It will never be finished, actually—homes evolve with the families who live in them.

Permit yourself to take time. Make thoughtful choices rather than hasty ones. Save for pieces you really love rather than filling spaces with things you'll want to replace later. Let rooms come together gradually as you find the right elements.

The best homes have a personality that develops over the years—collected pieces from travels, inherited items with family history, art acquired as it was discovered rather than bought all at once to fill walls. These meaningful objects tell the story of who lives there. That kind of authentic character takes time. Let it unfold.

The goal isn't a perfect magazine-ready home. It's a home that supports your life, reflects who you are, and makes you feel at peace when you walk through the door. That's worth waiting for.

A NOTE ON NEW-CONSTRUCTION DESIGN CENTERS

If you're buying a new construction, much of your design happens before you move in—at the builder's design center, where you select your finishes, upgrades, and options. This is an exciting appointment, but it can also be overwhelming and expensive if you're not prepared.

The most important distinction to understand is between structural options and cosmetic upgrades. Structural options—adding a bedroom, extending the garage, framing a bonus room, and roughing in plumbing for a future bathroom—must be selected during construction. You can't easily or affordably add these after the home is finished. Cosmetic upgrades—countertops, premium flooring, and more sophisticated light fixtures—can always be done later, often for less than the builder charges.

Prioritize the things you can't change after the fact. Set a budget before your design center appointment, know which structural options matter most to you, and don't get swept up in every cosmetic upgrade the designer shows you. You can always add the upgraded backsplash or premium carpet next year. You can't add a bathroom rough-in once the slab is poured.

•••RESOURCE•••

For more design ideas, tips, and inspiration as you settle into your new home, visit www.justinskeytohomelife.com. I regularly share content on making your home work better for your life—from simple weekend projects to bigger transformations—on the blog and across my social media channels.

While you're there, check out the EZRenovizer. This interactive home renovation visualizer lets you see what different flooring, countertops, cabinets, backsplash, fixtures, and lighting would actually look like in a space before you spend a dime. If you've ever stared at a tiny swatch in a showroom and tried to imagine how it would look across your entire kitchen floor, this tool takes the guesswork out of it.

There's a free seven-day trial so you can explore everything it offers with no commitment. If you love it—which I think you will—the monthly subscription is very affordable, and you can cancel anytime. It's one of those tools that can save you from expensive mistakes and give you the confidence to make design decisions you'll be happy with for years.

Your home is a journey, not a destination, and I'm here to help you enjoy every step of it.

CHAPTER 16
Planning Renovations That Add Value

• • •

At some point after buying your home, you'll probably want to make changes. Maybe immediately, to address things you knew needed updating when you bought. After living there for a while, you may discover what works and what doesn't. Your family's needs may evolve over time.

Some renovations add significant value—both to your daily enjoyment of the home and to its resale value when the time eventually comes to sell. Others cost more than they return, consuming money and effort for marginal benefit. Understanding the difference helps you make informed decisions about where to invest your renovation dollars.

RENOVATIONS WITH THE BEST RETURNS

Kitchen updates consistently rank among the best renovation investments. The kitchen is the heart of most homes—where families gather, where mornings start and evenings wind down, where you'll spend countless hours over the years. Buyers prioritize kitchens when evaluating homes, and a dated kitchen can sink an otherwise attractive property.

You don't necessarily need a complete gut renovation to see benefits. Sometimes modest updates make a dramatic difference: refinished or painted cabinet fronts, updated hardware, new countertops, modern fixtures and appliances, improved lighting. These changes can transform a dated kitchen at a fraction of the cost of a full remodel.

Bathroom remodels, especially in primary suites, also yield strong returns. Like kitchens, bathrooms are high-use spaces where outdated features are immediately obvious. Fresh tile, updated vanities, new fixtures, improved lighting, and better ventilation can modernize a bathroom without moving walls or plumbing.

Curb appeal improvements offer excellent returns for relatively modest investment. The exterior is the first thing anyone sees—visitors, neighbors, potential buyers. Landscaping upgrades, fresh exterior paint or power washing, a new front door, updated house numbers and exterior lighting, repaired walkways and driveways—these relatively small investments dramatically affect how the entire property is perceived.

Adding usable square footage—finishing a basement, converting an attic, or adding a room—can significantly increase value when done well. But costs vary widely based on existing conditions and local construction costs, so obtain multiple quotes and realistic assessments of value-addition before committing.

RENOVATIONS WITH POOR RETURNS

Swimming pools rarely recoup their installation costs and can actually reduce your pool's buyer pool (no pun intended) when selling. Many families don't want the maintenance burden, liability concerns, and ongoing costs associated with pools.

Over-improving for your neighborhood is a classic mistake. If you have the nicest house on the block by a wide margin, you've probably spent money you'll never recoup. Home values are heavily influenced by surrounding properties—your home's ceiling is partially determined by what neighboring homes sell for.

Highly personalized improvements may suit your specific taste but can hurt resale appeal. Unusual paint colors, niche custom features, unconventional layouts, and quirky design choices that appeal to you may turn off most prospective buyers.

Converting bedrooms to other uses—combining two bedrooms into one larger room, turning a bedroom into a massive closet—typically reduces value. Bedroom count is a primary sorting criterion for most home searches. A three-bedroom home reaches more buyers than a two-bedroom, regardless of overall square footage.

ENERGY EFFICIENCY UPGRADES

One category of renovation that deserves its own conversation is energy efficiency. These upgrades often fly under the radar because they aren't as exciting as a new kitchen, but they can save you real money every single month and make your home more attractive to future buyers.

Adding or upgrading insulation, especially in the attic, is one of the most cost-effective improvements you can make. Replacing old single-pane windows with energy-efficient models reduces heating and cooling costs and improves year-round comfort. Upgrading to a high-efficiency HVAC system can significantly reduce your energy bills, especially if your current system is fifteen or more years old.

Even small changes, such as installing a smart thermostat, sealing air leaks around doors and windows, and switching to light-emitting diode (LED) lighting throughout the home, add up over time.

Many of these upgrades qualify for federal tax credits or local utility rebates, which can offset a meaningful portion of the cost. Check what's available in your area before you start—you might be surprised at how much you can save on the front end.

PLANNING YOUR PROJECTS

Before starting any renovation, define your goals clearly. Are you improving purely for your own enjoyment with no concern for resale impact? Are you preparing to sell in the near future and want to maximize your return? Are you planning to stay long-term but want to build equity along the way? Different goals suggest different priorities and approaches.

Get multiple bids—at least three—for any significant project. Prices can vary dramatically between contractors for the same work. Multiple bids help you understand what's reasonable and identify outliers in either direction.

Build contingency into your budget. Projects almost always cost more than initial estimates once work begins and hidden conditions are discovered. Budget 15 to 20 percent above quoted prices to handle surprises without stress.

Consider phasing larger projects rather than doing everything at once. Spreading work over time makes the financial burden more manageable and lets you learn from each phase before tackling the next. You might also discover that some planned changes aren't actually necessary once you've lived with earlier improvements.

Document everything. Take photos before, during, and after. Keep all contracts, receipts, permits, and warranties. This protects you throughout the project and provides valuable records for future owners or insurers.

PERMITS AND CODE COMPLIANCE

Before any significant renovation begins, find out whether you need a permit. Most work that involves structural changes, electrical, plumbing, HVAC, or additions requires one. Your local building department or county permitting office can tell you exactly what applies to your project.

Don't skip permits to save time or money. Unpermitted work can create serious problems. Your homeowner's insurance may not cover damage related to work that wasn't properly permitted and inspected. When you go to sell, unpermitted additions or modifications can derail a transaction—buyers' lenders and inspectors will flag them, and you may be forced to tear out work, bring it up to code, or reduce your asking price. Permits ensure work is done safely and correctly. They protect you now, and they protect you later.

HIRING THE RIGHT CONTRACTOR

The contractor you hire will make or break your renovation experience. A good contractor delivers quality work within a reasonable timeframe and at a fair price. A bad one can turn a straightforward project into a nightmare that costs you far more than it should have.

Start with the basics. Make sure they're licensed and insured—ask to see proof of both. Check references and actually call them. Review photos of past work and, if possible, visit a completed project in person. Get everything in writing before work begins: scope of work, timeline, payment schedule, materials to be used, and how changes will be handled. A reputable contractor will have no problem putting it all on paper.

Watch for red flags. A contractor who demands full payment upfront, won't provide a written contract, can't show proof of insurance, has no references, or won't share them, or pressures you to make a decision immediately—these are signs to walk away.

One detail I can't stress enough is getting an itemized list of the specific materials that will be used in your project. Not just "kitchen faucet" or "bathroom vanity"—the actual brand, model, and finish. This matters more than most people realize, and I learned this the hard way myself.

A little over three years ago, I renovated my kitchen, a full bathroom, the living room, dining room, hallway, and foyer, and replaced the railing in my home. I'd have done most, if not all, of the work myself, but my wife was pregnant with our son at the time, and between my work schedule and preparing for a growing family, I didn't have the time. We needed the work done to make our home function better for our life ahead.

So I hired a company to do it. I followed all the same advice I'm giving you right now—multiple bids, written contracts, references, the whole process. But I didn't follow my own advice about getting an itemized list of the exact materials that would be used. The company did a great job overall, but they installed plumbing faucets that looked similar to what we had selected, but were of very low quality. Within six months, the finish began to peel. Fortunately, it wasn't a high cost to replace them, but it was a frustrating lesson. Even with nearly three decades in this industry, I got caught skipping a step I knew better than to skip. Don't make the same mistake. Get that itemized list. Review it. Approve it before work begins.

DIY VS. HIRING A PROFESSIONAL

There are projects you can absolutely handle yourself, and there are projects where hiring a professional isn't just the smarter choice—it's the safer one.

Painting, swapping out cabinet hardware, replacing light fixtures, updating landscaping, installing a new faucet, building shelving—these are all reasonable DIY projects for most homeowners with basic tools and a willingness to learn. There are countless tutorials available, and the risk of a serious mistake is low. The worst that usually happens is that it takes longer than you expected or that you need a second trip to the hardware store.

Electrical work, plumbing beyond simple fixture swaps, structural modifications, roofing, and anything that requires a permit—these should be left to licensed professionals. The consequences of getting these wrong are beyond cosmetic. Bad electrical work is a fire hazard. Improper plumbing can cause water damage that costs thousands to repair. Structural mistakes can compromise your home's safety. And a bad DIY job almost always costs more to fix than hiring a professional would have cost in the first place. Know your limits, and don't let pride or a desire to save money put your family or your investment at risk.

WHAT I'VE SEEN GO RIGHT AND WRONG

After nearly three decades in this industry, I've seen families handle renovations beautifully, and I've seen them make costly mistakes. The ones who do it well almost always share the same traits: they plan before they start, they set realistic budgets with contingency built in, they hire qualified people, and they prioritize the projects that matter most rather than trying to do everything at once.

Costly mistakes usually result from rushing. I've seen families gut an entire kitchen when new countertops, fresh paint, and updated hardware would have transformed the space at a fraction of the cost. I've seen homeowners skip permits to save a few hundred dollars, only to face thousands in problems when they went to sell. I've seen people hire the lowest bidder without checking references and end up paying twice—once for the poor work and again to have it fixed. Take your time, do your homework, and approach renovations as investments, not impulses.

Your home will evolve, and that's a good thing. Every renovation is a chance to make it work better for your life. Just be smart about it. Plan carefully, hire the right people, protect yourself with permits and documentation, and spend your money where it matters most. Do that, and every dollar you invest in your home will be a dollar well spent.

• • • RESOURCE • • •

If you're planning a renovation and want to see what different finishes and materials would look like before you commit, head over to www.justinskeytohomelife.com and check out the EZRenovizer. It lets you visualize changes to flooring, countertops, cabinets, tile, fixtures, and more, so you can make confident decisions before you spend a dollar. There's a free seven-day trial, the monthly subscription is very affordable, and you can cancel at any time. It's one of the best tools I can offer to take the guesswork out of renovation planning.

CHAPTER 17

Budget-Friendly Upgrades

• • •

Not every improvement requires a contractor or a substantial budget. Some of the most impactful changes you can make to your home cost very little—just time, effort, and attention to detail.

These budget-friendly upgrades won't transform a fundamentally problematic home into a dream house. But in a well-designed home, they can make a dramatic difference in how spaces look and feel. They're especially valuable in the early years of homeownership when budgets are often tightest.

THE POWER OF PAINT

Nothing transforms a room faster or more affordably than fresh paint. New paint makes old walls look new again, covers countless minor imperfections, and can completely change the feel of a space—from dark and cramped to light and open, from cold and sterile to warm and inviting.

Don't underestimate the importance of preparation. The work you do before the brush touches the wall affects the final result more than most people realize. Clean the walls thoroughly. Fill holes and cracks with spackle and sand them smooth. Then tape off trim, ceilings, and anything you don't want painted. Use quality primer where needed, especially over dark colors, new drywall, or stains.

When choosing colors, if you have any doubts, go lighter rather than darker. Dark colors can work beautifully, but are harder to get right and can make spaces feel smaller. Light neutrals make rooms feel larger, brighter, and more versatile as décor changes over time. You can always add color through accessories if neutrals feel too bland.

Don't forget the trim. Fresh white trim makes everything look cleaner, crisper, and more finished. Painting trim is tedious work—lots of detail, lots of taping, lots of careful cutting in—but the impact is substantial. Crisp white trim against fresh wall color creates a polished, intentional look.

HARDWARE AND FIXTURES

Small hardware elements have a significant visual impact at minimal cost. Cabinet knobs and pulls, drawer handles, door knobs, hinges, light switch plates, outlet covers, towel bars, toilet paper holders—these small items collectively define the feel of a room.

Dated brass hardware from the 1990s screams "not updated," even if everything else looks fine. Swapping it for brushed nickel, matte black, or oil-rubbed bronze instantly modernizes spaces. Mismatched finishes (brushed nickel here, chrome there, brass somewhere else) look chaotic; consistent finishes look intentional and coordinated.

This is one of the easiest upgrades to tackle yourself. Unscrew old hardware, screw in new hardware. If hole patterns match, it takes minutes per item. Even if you need to drill new holes, it's straightforward work that most homeowners can handle.

Don't overlook interior doors and door hardware. Replacing hollow-core doors with solid-core or panel doors adds a noticeable quality upgrade, but even just updating the doorknobs and hinges to a matching modern finish can change the feel of a hallway. The same goes for bathroom accessories—towel bars, robe hooks, toilet paper holders, and towel rings. When these elements match and complement the faucet finish, the bathroom feels coordinated and intentional. When the space has a random mix of chrome, brass, and plastic, it feels neglected, no matter how clean it is.

LIGHTING UPGRADES

Outdated light fixtures date a home more obviously than almost anything else. That brass chandelier in the dining room, the builder-grade flush mounts in the hallways, the bare bulb in the closet—they all announce "this home hasn't been updated."

Replacing fixtures can dramatically transform rooms. A statement pendant over a kitchen island or dining table. Modern ceiling fans with integrated lights. Coordinated bathroom vanity lighting. Updated flush mounts or semi-flush fixtures in hallways and bedrooms.

Add dimmer switches to any room where you want mood flexibility. Dimmers are inexpensive, relatively easy to install if you're comfortable with basic electrical work, and let you shift a room from bright task lighting to cozy evening ambiance with a simple adjustment.

Consider adding light sources to dark corners. Floor lamps and table lamps are obvious additions, but don't overlook under-cabinet lighting in kitchens, picture lights over artwork, and night lights in hallways. Most rooms are actually under-lit for the activities that happen in them.

Don't forget the bulbs themselves. Switching to LED bulbs throughout your home reduces your electric bill and lets you choose the right color temperature for each space. Warm white for living areas and bedrooms to create a cozy feel. Brighter, cooler tones for kitchens, bathrooms, and workspaces where clear visibility is essential. It's a small change most people overlook, but once you get the lighting right in a room, everything else in that room looks better as well.

LANDSCAPING REFRESHES

Curb appeal matters, and basic landscaping improvements require more sweat than dollars.

Fresh mulch instantly improves the appearance of planting beds. It suppresses weeds, retains moisture, and makes everything look tidier and more maintained. A few cubic yards of mulch and a couple of hours of spreading can transform your home's exterior.

Trimmed bushes and edged beds make the difference between "maintained" and "neglected." Overgrown shrubs blocking windows, grass encroaching into beds, straggly plants that haven't been shaped—these signal deferred maintenance even if everything else is fine.

A few seasonal flowers add color and life without major investment. Container gardens by the front door, simple annuals in visible beds, a hanging basket or two—these touches make a home feel cared for and welcoming.

You don't need elaborate landscaping to make an impact. Simple and well-maintained beats complex and neglected every single time.

DEEP CLEANING AND MAINTENANCE

Sometimes a home doesn't need changing—it just needs cleaning. Professional deep cleaning services can tackle issues that regular maintenance doesn't cover.

Carpet cleaning removes years of accumulated dirt and stains, brightening rooms and eliminating odors. Pressure washing exterior surfaces—siding, decks, patios, driveways—removes grime and mildew that dulls their appearance. Window cleaning, inside and out, lets in more light and improves views.

Attention to cleaning details matters too. Scrubbing grout until it's actually white again. Polishing fixtures until they shine. Cleaning light fixtures and ceiling fan blades. Washing baseboards and door frames. These aren't glamorous tasks, but they make everything look better.

Before spending money to replace items, consider whether cleaning them is sufficient. Sometimes what looks worn out is actually just dirty.

WINDOW TREATMENTS

Dated blinds and curtains can make an otherwise updated room look tired. Cracked plastic mini-blinds, dusty vertical blinds, or faded curtains that have been hanging since the previous owner lived there—these are the kind of details that quietly drag a room down without you even realizing it until they're replaced.

One simple trick that makes a big difference is hanging curtain rods higher and wider than the window frame. Mounting the rod close to the ceiling and extending it several inches beyond the window on each side makes the window appear larger and the room feel taller. Use floor-length curtains for a clean, finished look. You don't need expensive fabric to pull this off—there are affordable options at nearly every home store that look far more expensive than they actually are. This one change can elevate a room from basic to polished for under $50 per window.

CAULK AND GROUT REFRESH

This is one of the most overlooked and cheapest improvements you can make. Peeling, yellowed, or mildewed caulk around bathtubs, showers, sinks, and countertops looks unsightly and can allow moisture to penetrate where it shouldn't. Removing old caulk and applying a fresh, clean bead takes about an hour per area and costs just a few dollars in materials. The visual difference is immediate.

Grout is the same story. Stained or discolored grout makes tile look old and dirty, even if the tile itself is in perfect condition. A grout pen can restore the color for a few dollars. For more significant discoloration, re-grouting a bathroom floor or shower wall is a weekend project that makes the space look practically new. If you've ever walked into a bathroom and felt like something was off but couldn't quite place it, there's a good chance it was the grout.

SHELVING AND ORGANIZATION

An organized home feels bigger and functions better, even without adding a single square foot. Closets are the most common pain point. Most homes come with a single shelf and a rod, which wastes significant usable space. Affordable closet organizer kits from any home-improvement store can double or triple your storage capacity and make a cluttered closet look like something out of a magazine.

The same principle applies to pantries, garages, and laundry rooms. Simple shelving, clear storage bins, and a system that keeps everything in its logical place can transform chaotic spaces into functional ones. The investment is minimal, and the daily quality-of-life improvement is significant. When everything has a place, the whole house feels calmer and more manageable.

Floating shelves are another affordable addition worth considering. In kitchens, bathrooms, or living areas, a set of well-placed floating shelves adds both storage and visual interest. They're relatively easy to install and provide a place to display items that would otherwise clutter countertops or sit in a box. Organization is one of those upgrades that didn't photograph well for a listing, but buyers notice it the moment they open a closet door. A well-organized home signals to prospective buyers that the property has been well-maintained and cared for.

SMART-HOME ADDITIONS ON A BUDGET

You don't need to wire your entire house to start enjoying smart-home technology. There are affordable entry points that add real convenience to your daily life and appeal to future buyers when the time comes to sell.

A smart thermostat is a strong starting point. It learns your schedule, adjusts temperatures automatically, and can reduce your energy bills while giving you control from your phone. A video doorbell lets you see who's at your door from anywhere, which adds both convenience and security. Smart plugs let you control lamps, fans, and small appliances with your voice or phone for just a few dollars per plug. Smart lighting lets you set schedules, adjust brightness, and change color temperature to match the time of day. None of these require professional installation, and all of them make your home feel more modern and connected. Start with one or two and build from there as your budget allows.

THE UPGRADES I ALWAYS RECOMMEND

After nearly three decades of walking through homes with families, I recommend a handful of budget-friendly upgrades to almost everyone. Fresh paint in the rooms you use most. Updated hardware throughout the home in a consistent finish. At least one or two updated light fixtures in the spaces where outdated ones are most obvious. Fresh caulk in every bathroom and kitchen. And clean, well-maintained landscaping out front.

These are the changes that consistently deliver the greatest impact for the least cost. You don't need to do them all at once. Pick the one that will make the most impact in your home right now and start there. Then work your way through the list as time and budget allow. The cumulative effect of several small, affordable improvements often rivals that of a single expensive renovation.

• • • RESOURCE • • •

For more budget-friendly project ideas, step-by-step guides, and tools to help you visualize changes before you commit to them, visit www.justinskeytohomelife.com. Making your home better didn't have to break the bank, and I continually add new content to help you get the most out of every dollar you invest in the place you call home.

CHAPTER 18

Working with Contractors

• • •

For projects beyond your DIY skill level—and honestly, you should be realistic about what that level is—you'll need to hire professionals. How you find, evaluate, hire, and manage contractors determines whether you get quality work at a fair price or end up frustrated, over budget, and underwhelmed.

Good contractors are valuable partners who can transform your home. Bad ones can waste your money, damage your property, and create years of headaches. Learning to tell the difference is one of the most important skills a homeowner can develop.

FINDING GOOD CONTRACTORS

Word of mouth remains your best resource for finding quality contractors. Ask neighbors, coworkers, friends, and family members who've recently done similar projects. Personal recommendations from people who've seen the completed work and experienced the working relationship are worth more than any advertisement or online listing.

When gathering recommendations, ask specifically what they liked and didn't like about working with that contractor. Ask whether the project finished on time and on budget. Ask whether there were any surprises or problems and how they were handled. Ask whether they'd hire the contractor again without hesitation.

Check credentials before engaging further. Licensed contractors have demonstrated at least minimum competency and are accountable to licensing boards if problems arise. Insured contractors protect you from liability if someone gets hurt on your property. Request current documentation for both. Most states have online databases where you can verify a contractor's license status and check for complaints or disciplinary actions—take five minutes and look them up. Make sure they carry both general liability insurance and workers' compensation coverage. If an uninsured worker is injured on your property, you could be held financially responsible.

Get at least three quotes for any significant project. This helps you understand what's reasonable for the work involved and identifies outliers in either direction. If one bid is dramatically lower than others, ask yourself why—they may be cutting corners, using inferior materials, or not fully understanding the scope.

GETTING USEFUL QUOTES

For quotes to be useful for comparison, they need to specify the same scope. A vague quote that says "remodel bathroom" could mean many different things. A detailed quote that specifies exactly what's included—demolition of existing fixtures, installation of specified tub-shower, vanity, toilet, tile work with grout color, painting, and so on—can actually be compared against other quotes.

When getting quotes, provide the same information to each contractor. Walk through the project scope in detail. Show them the space. Discuss your expectations and timeline. Answer their questions fully. Inconsistent information leads to inconsistent quotes that can't be meaningfully compared.

Pay attention to what's explicitly excluded. Does the quote include permits? Debris removal? Painting around the new work? Moving furniture? Fixing unexpected problems discovered once work begins? Assumptions about what's included lead to disputes later.

The lowest quote isn't automatically the best choice. Consider the contractor's reputation, communication style, timeline, and your confidence in their ability to deliver quality work. A slightly higher quote from someone you trust may be the better investment.

MANAGING THE PROJECT

Once you've selected a contractor, get everything in writing before work begins. The contract should specify exactly what work will be performed, which materials will be used, the timeline, the payment schedule, how changes will be handled, and the applicable warranties.

Never pay everything upfront. A typical payment structure might be a deposit to secure the job and order materials (usually 10 to 30 percent), progress payments at defined milestones, and final payment upon completion and your satisfaction. Never make the final payment until all work is complete and inspected.

Maintain clear communication throughout the project. Establish how and when you'll discuss progress, questions, and decisions.

Be available when needed, but don't micromanage—let professionals do their work without constant hovering.

Document everything. Keep copies of contracts, change orders, permits, and communications. Take photos before, during, and after construction. This documentation protects you in the event of disputes and provides valuable records for future reference.

Expect some disruption and inconvenience. Construction is messy and disruptive, even when it goes well. Things may take longer than planned. Unexpected issues may arise. Patience and flexibility help everyone involved.

CHANGE ORDERS AND SCOPE CREEP

Once a project is underway, you'll almost certainly want to make changes. Maybe you see the space taking shape and realize you want a different layout. Maybe you find a fixture you prefer to the one you originally selected. Maybe the contractor opens a wall and discovers something that changes the plan. These are all normal, but every change has a cost and an impact on the timeline.

Any change to the original scope of work should be documented in a written change order before the work happens. The change order should describe what's being added, removed, or modified, the cost impact, and any effect on the timeline. Both you and the contractor should sign it. This protects both parties and prevents the kind of disagreements that happen when someone says, "I thought that was included," and the other says, "That was never part of the deal."

Watch out for the "while you're at it" trap. It's easy to keep adding features once work is in progress—while you're at it, let's replace that flooring, add recessed lights, and redo the closet. Each one seems small on its own, but they stack up fast. Before you know it, your budget has doubled, and the project that was supposed to take three weeks is going on for two months. Be disciplined about what you add and make sure every change is something you genuinely need, not just something convenient because the crew is already there.

LIVING THROUGH A RENOVATION

If you're living in the home while work is being done, plan for it. Renovations are disruptive to daily life, and a little preparation goes a long way toward keeping your sanity.

If the kitchen is being renovated, set up a temporary kitchen area somewhere else in your house. A microwave, a coffee maker, paper plates, and a mini fridge or cooler can get you through more than you think. If you have the space and budget to plan ahead, it's worth establishing something more permanent before the renovation begins.

That's exactly what I did. About a year before my main renovation, I added a ten-foot wet bar in my basement with a large single-bowl sink and two undercounter refrigerators. When the kitchen renovation started, that basement setup became our temporary kitchen, and it was a lifesaver for our family. Our main renovation—kitchen, full bathroom, living room, dining room, hallway, foyer, and railing—took about a month and a half from demolition to completion. Having that functioning space downstairs meant my family could still eat real meals, keep food cold, and wash dishes without relying on takeout every night or fighting over a bathroom sink. If you know a big renovation is coming, think about what you can put in place ahead of time to make life livable while the work is being done.

As it turned out, the renovation was completed on the same day my amazing son was born. That's something I'll never forget—walking into a brand-new home and a brand-new chapter of life all at once. I have to give credit to my wife for being absolutely amazing through all of it. Living in a construction zone while pregnant, dealing with the noise, the dust, the disruption to our daily routine—she handled it with more patience and grace than I probably deserved. We both just kept our eyes on the future and the quality-of-life improvements the finished home would bring our family. That shared vision made the temporary inconvenience worth every bit.

Dust and debris are the biggest daily challenges during a renovation. Construction dust gets everywhere if you don't take steps to contain it. I had the HVAC vents in the work area temporarily sealed to prevent dust from being pulled into the system and blown throughout the rest of the house. We also put up a plastic doorway barrier with a zipper door opening between the construction zone and our living space. That zipper door made a huge difference—the crew could move in and out easily, but the dust and debris stayed contained on their side. Without those two steps, every room in the house would have been coated in a fine layer of drywall dust and sawdust within the first week.

Move valuables and fragile items away from the construction zone before work begins. Cover furniture and electronics in adjacent rooms with drop cloths or plastic. If you have young children or pets, figure out how to keep them safely away from the work area, open tools, and exposed wiring or plumbing. Talk to your contractor about daily start and stop times, where the crew will park, which entrances they'll use, and how the workspace will be left at the end of each day. A renovation that lasts a month or more isn't just a construction project—it is a disruption to your family's daily routine. The more you plan for that reality upfront, the smoother the experience will be for everyone.

One device that worked really well for us was using our Kwikset smart lock on the front door to manage contractor access. We gave the crew their own entry code and restricted the hours it would work, so they could come and go during the agreed-upon work schedule without us needing to be home to let them in. When the project was finished, we deleted their code. No worrying about whether someone made copies of a house key, no awkward conversations about returning keys. Not that anyone we hired would have done anything wrong—they were fantastic people. But a smart lock gives you control and peace of mind, and it's one of those small investments in technology that pays for itself in convenience the first time you use it for something like this.

RED FLAGS TO WATCH FOR

Certain warning signs should make you cautious or prompt you to seek another contractor.

Demanding cash only or refusing to provide receipts suggests someone is operating outside normal business practices. Legitimate contractors accept various payment methods and document their transactions.

No written contract or resistance to putting things in writing? Professionals understand that documentation protects both parties. Unwillingness to formalize agreements suggests problems ahead.

Pressure to decide immediately or claims that a price is only good today? Quality contractors have enough work that they don't need high-pressure tactics. Artificial urgency is a manipulation technique. I experienced this firsthand when we replaced our roof right after buying our home. I met with six roofing companies, and three of them used the "this price is only good today if you sign right here" tactic. With my background in this industry, I have zero tolerance for that approach. To me, it's an immediate red flag for a company I don't want to work with. I rejected all three on the spot and explained why.

The company I ultimately chose never pressured me. They had great references, which I called. They itemized everything on paper. They weren't the cheapest option, but they were the best option. That distinction matters. Cheapest isn't always best, and anyone who tries to rush you into a decision is hoping you won't take the time to find out.

Bids significantly lower than competitors' bids, without a clear explanation, are also a concern. Either they're cutting corners, using inferior materials, or planning to raise the price once you're committed.

Unable or unwilling to provide references? Good contractors have satisfied customers willing to vouch for their work. A lack of references suggests there are no satisfied customers.

Trust your instincts. If something feels wrong about a contractor—their communication, their attitude, their workspace behavior—it probably is. Moving on to find someone better is always an option until contracts are signed.

WHEN THINGS GO WRONG

Even with the best planning, problems can arise. Materials arrive damaged. Work didn't meet your expectations. Timelines slip beyond what was agreed to. How you handle these situations matters.

Start with direct communication. Most issues can be resolved by having an honest conversation with your contractor. Point out what you see, reference the contract or change order, and allow them to make it right. Good contractors want to deliver quality work and will address legitimate concerns without pushback. Document everything in writing. Even if you discuss it in person, follow up with a text or email summarizing the agreed-upon points.

If direct communication didn't resolve the issue, your written contract is your protection. This is exactly why everything must be in writing before work begins. If the contractor isn't meeting the terms of the contract, you have the right to withhold final payment until the work is completed to the agreed standard. If the situation escalates beyond what you can resolve together, you can file a complaint with your state's licensing board or consult with an attorney. These are last resorts, but knowing they exist gives you leverage and protection.

TIMELINE EXPECTATIONS

Projects almost always take longer than the original estimate. This isn't necessarily a sign that something is wrong—it is just the reality of construction work. Weather can delay exterior projects. Materials get backordered. Subcontractors have scheduling conflicts. Inspectors aren't always available on the day you need them. One delay early in the process can push everything else back.

Build extra time into your expectations, just as you build contingency into your budget. If the contractor says three weeks, mentally plan for four or five. If they say six weeks, prepare for eight. This isn't pessimism—it is realistic planning that saves you from unnecessary frustration. When the project finishes on time, you'll be pleasantly surprised. When it runs a little long, you won't be caught off guard.

That said, a good contractor should communicate proactively when delays happen. If you aren't hearing from them and the timeline is slipping, that's worth a direct conversation. Delays happen—silence about delays should not. You deserve to know where your project stands, what caused the setback, and what the revised timeline looks like. A contractor who keeps you informed, even when the news isn't great, is one worth working with again.

WHAT I'VE LEARNED FROM THE OTHER SIDE

Having spent nearly three decades working alongside builders and contractors in the housing industry, I've seen the full range of crews, from those who take extraordinary pride in their work to those who cut every corner. The best contractors I've worked with all share the same traits: they communicate clearly, they show up when they say they will, they stand behind their work, and they treat your home like it matters to them because it does.

The ones who cause problems almost always show warning signs early. They're hard to reach before the job starts. They're vague about details. They resist putting things in writing. They talk over you instead of listening to what you want. Pay attention to how a contractor treats you during the quoting process because that's exactly how they'll treat you during the project. If you feel respected, heard, and informed before the first nail is driven, you're probably in good hands. If you feel rushed, dismissed, or confused, find someone else.

For contractor checklists, project planning guides, and more resources to help you navigate your next renovation, visit www.justinskeytohomelife.com.

• • •

CONTRACTOR VETTING CHECKLIST

• • •

- ☐ Licensed in your state?
- ☐ Insured and bonded?
- ☐ In business for at least three to five years?
- ☐ Willing to provide three or more recent references?
- ☐ Written detailed estimate provided?
- ☐ Payment schedule reasonable? (Never more than 10 percent upfront.)
- ☐ Contract includes scope, materials, timeline, and warranty?

• • • WATCH OUT • • •

Never pay more than 10 percent upfront. A legitimate contractor can buy materials on account. Large upfront payments protect the contractor, not you. Pay in stages tied to completed milestones, with final payment held until the work passes inspection and you're satisfied.

CHAPTER 19
Creating Outdoor Living Spaces

• • •

Your home doesn't end where the walls do. Outdoor spaces extend your living area, provide places for relaxation and entertainment, and connect you with nature, fresh air, and neighbors. A well-designed outdoor area can feel like adding rooms to your home—without the cost and complexity of actual construction.

Whether you have a small patio, a large backyard, or something in between, thoughtful development of outdoor spaces significantly enhances both your daily enjoyment and your home's value.

DECKS AND PATIOS

A deck or patio is the foundation of most outdoor living spaces—the platform from which everything else extends. Getting it right in size, location, and materials sets up everything that follows.

Consider how you'll actually use the space. Space to dine requires tables and chairs with adequate clearance around them. Space for relaxation requires comfortable seating arrangements. Entertaining means room for people to move, mingle, and gather. Outdoor cooking needs a designated grill area with appropriate clearances and surfaces. Think through your likely uses before committing to dimensions.

Think about traffic flow from indoors to out. The transition should feel natural and convenient, not awkward or distant. Access directly from the kitchen or family room usually works best—you'll use outdoor spaces more when they're easy to reach and service.

Materials matter for both appearance and long-term maintenance. Wood decks offer a traditional warm appearance but require regular sealing, staining, and eventual board replacement. Composite materials cost more upfront but resist rot, insects, and fading with minimal upkeep. Concrete patios are durable and low-maintenance, but can crack over time. Pavers offer design flexibility and allow easy repair of individual units, but they may shift or allow weed growth between units. When comparing costs, factor in long-term maintenance costs, not just the installation price. A composite deck that costs more to build but needs almost no upkeep over twenty years may end up being cheaper than a wood deck you have to stain and seal every two years.

Keep in mind that decks and patios often require permits, especially if they're attached to the house, elevated above a certain height, or include electrical or plumbing work. Check with your local building department before you start. As I mentioned in the renovation chapters, skipping permits is never worth the risk.

When I replaced the failing deck outside my home, I followed the same process I've recommended throughout this book. I got multiple bids, checked references, and hired a great company to do the work. During the planning process, they tried to talk me into using a cheaper composite decking material than the one I had selected, which I genuinely appreciated—they were trying to save me money while still providing a good, low-maintenance option. But I had done my research and knew what I wanted. Some composite deck boards can flex underfoot when you walk on them, and that was something I wasn't willing to live with. I chose a high-end composite board that felt solid, and I've never regretted it.

I also had a gutter system installed underneath the deck so that rainwater would be channeled away rather than draining straight through. That allowed me to add a paver brick patio below the deck, creating an additional usable living space for my family—one we can enjoy even when it's raining. It has been great for our family. That lower patio essentially gave us a covered outdoor room without the cost of building an entirely separate structure. If your deck is elevated enough to allow usable space underneath, it's worth exploring this option. The gutter system is a relatively small addition during the deck build, but it unlocks a whole second level of outdoor living.

Also, consider shade. A beautiful deck or patio that bakes in direct summer sun is miserable to use during the hottest parts of the day. Umbrellas, pergolas, shade sails, retractable awnings, or strategically placed trees extend the usable hours of your outdoor space.

LANDSCAPING FOR LIVING

Good landscaping isn't just decorative—it shapes spaces, creates privacy, provides shade, manages views, and establishes atmosphere. Think of landscaping as the walls and ceiling of your outdoor rooms.

Consider sight lines from both inside and outside your home. What do you see from key windows? What do neighbors see of you? What views would you like to enhance or screen? Strategic planting can frame attractive views, hide unsightly ones, and create privacy without feeling like a fortress.

Create distinct zones within your outdoor space. A lawn area for kids to play. A garden bed to tend. A quiet corner for morning coffee or evening relaxation. A fire pit area for gathering. Different zones serving different purposes make the outdoor spaces more usable and interesting than a single undifferentiated area.

Consider maintenance requirements honestly. That elaborate garden you envision will only look good if you're actually willing and able to maintain it. Most homeowners do better with simpler landscapes they can realistically maintain than with ambitious designs that deteriorate into overgrown messes.

Consider using native plants that are adapted to your region's climate and soil. They typically require less watering, less fertilizer, and less ongoing care than non-native species while supporting local pollinators and wildlife. A local garden center can point you toward varieties that thrive in your area without constant attention.

Also, pay attention to drainage. Landscaping that directs water toward your foundation instead of away from it can lead to serious moisture problems in your basement or crawl space. Make sure your grading slopes away from the house and that downspouts extend far enough to move water clear of the foundation.

OUTDOOR COMFORT FEATURES

Several features make outdoor spaces more comfortable and usable across a wider range of conditions.

Shade is essential, as mentioned. Plan for it from the start rather than enduring hot summers and adding it later.

Outdoor lighting extends use into evening hours and improves safety. Path lighting guides movement and prevents trips. Ambient lighting creates an atmosphere for dining and relaxing. Task lighting illuminates cooking and work areas. Consider solar options for easy installation without running electrical circuits.

Weather-resistant furniture is worth the investment. Cheap furniture that rusts, fades, or falls apart after one season costs more in the long run than quality pieces that last a decade or more. Bring cushions inside or store them properly to extend their life.

Consider heating options for cool evenings. Fire pits create natural gathering spots. Outdoor heaters extend patio season into fall or early spring. Even simple fire bowls with gel fuel add warmth and ambiance.

Privacy features—whether fencing, plantings, or screens—let you relax without feeling on display. Most people use outdoor spaces more when they feel comfortably secluded.

OUTDOOR KITCHENS AND COOKING AREAS

Outdoor cooking has come a long way from a standalone grill on a concrete pad. If your family spends a lot of time outside and you enjoy cooking and entertaining, an outdoor kitchen can be one of the most used and most loved features of your home.

It didn't have to be elaborate to be effective. A built-in grill with some countertop space on either side gives you room to prep and plate without running back and forth to the indoor kitchen. Add a small outdoor refrigerator, and you have cold drinks and ingredients within arm's reach. A sink with running water makes cleanup easier and prevents grease and mess from tracking through the house. Some families go even further with pizza ovens, smokers, built-in storage, and bar seating, but start with what you'll actually use. The best outdoor kitchen is the one that matches how your family lives, not the one that looks best in a magazine.

Placement matters. If your outdoor cooking area is too far from the indoor kitchen, you'll spend the whole time running back and forth for forgotten utensils, seasonings, and side dishes. Position it close enough that the two kitchens work together rather than compete. Make sure you have access to the utilities you need—gas lines for a built-in grill, water lines for a sink, and electrical outlets for lighting and small appliances. Planning these connections before construction begins saves money and reduces headaches compared to adding them later.

DESIGNING FOR KIDS AND PETS

If you have children or pets, your outdoor space needs to work for them too. That means thinking about safety, durability, and visibility.

Fencing is usually the priority. A securely fenced yard gives kids a safe place to play and gives dogs room to run without you worrying about them going onto the street. Make sure gates latch properly and that there are no gaps a small child or pet could squeeze through.

Choose surfaces that can handle heavy use—natural grass takes a beating from kids and dogs, so consider areas of mulch, rubber playground surfacing, or artificial turf in high-traffic zones.

Most importantly, design your outdoor space so you can see the play area from inside the house. Being able to watch your kids through the kitchen window while you're cooking dinner or cleaning up isn't a luxury—it is a practical necessity that will shape how much you actually use the yard.

This past year, I put in a Gorilla playset in our backyard for my son's birthday, and the decisions we made during that process are a perfect example of thinking through safety, materials, and placement. We installed a four-inch-tall robust rubber border around the playset and filled the entire area with four inches of playground mulch. This isn't regular mulch—it is very fine, so there are no splinters to worry about. We chose it over rubber mulch because it looks more natural in the yard and is probably a better landing surface if he takes a fall, which every kid eventually does. We built it in our fenced backyard and positioned it so we can see the entire playset from our kitchen window. Our son is still too young for us to leave him alone, so we're always right there with him when he plays. However, as he gets older, knowing we can glance out the window and see exactly what he's doing gives us real peace of mind. Every decision came back to the same question: Is this safe for our son and easy for us to monitor? If you're adding a play area to your yard, I'd encourage you to start with that same question.

EXTENDING YOUR OUTDOOR SEASON

In most parts of the country, outdoor spaces remain unused for several months of the year due to heat, cold, rain, or insects. Every feature that extends your usable season increases the return on your outdoor investment.

A screened porch keeps bugs out while letting in breezes, which can add two or three months of comfortable use during the warmer seasons. A covered patio or pergola with a solid roof lets you sit outside even in light rain and provides shade during the hottest part of the day. Fire pits and outdoor fireplaces make fall and early spring evenings enjoyable rather than just tolerable. There's something about gathering around a fire that draws a family together in a way nothing else quite does.

For families who want to extend the season, a three-season room with screens that can be swapped for glass panels bridges the gap between fully outdoor and fully indoor living. Think about how many months of the year your outdoor space will realistically be used and invest in the features that extend that number.

SMART OUTDOOR TECHNOLOGY

The same smart-home technology that makes life easier inside your home can enhance your outdoor spaces, too. Outdoor smart lighting lets you control your patio, pathway, and landscape lights from your phone, or set them to schedules so they turn on at sunset and off at bedtime. Weatherproof outdoor speakers let you play music throughout the yard without running wires or dragging portable speakers outside. And placing a Wi-Fi extender or mesh network node near an exterior wall ensures you have a strong signal on the patio, which matters more than you think when you're streaming music, using a baby monitor, or checking your security cameras.

Speaking of security cameras, outdoor cameras at entry points and around your property's perimeter provide peace of mind and a record of any incidents. I learned this lesson the hard way. Before I renovated our home, it was broken into. We never found out who did it. When the police crime lab came out and dusted for fingerprints, one of the first questions they asked was, "Do you have cameras?" I didn't. That moment made me realize how important it would be to add them.

My home is in a safe area, but crime happens everywhere. When it happens to you, you feel very violated. It changes the way you think about your home and your family's security. Since then, I've installed cameras both inside and outside some areas of our house. My family has joked that I've turned into Jason Bourne, which is very funny, but the peace of mind is real. Cameras aren't for everyone, and I understand that. But they work well for my family, and if you've ever had that feeling of wondering what happened while you were away, they're worth considering.

Finally, smart irrigation systems water your lawn and garden on optimized schedules based on weather and soil conditions, saving water and keeping your landscaping healthy without you having to stand in the yard with a hose. None of these outdoor technologies is expensive or complicated to set up, and each one makes your outdoor living experience a little more convenient and enjoyable.

WHAT FAMILIES ACTUALLY USE

After nearly three decades of working with families and their homes, I can tell you which outdoor features get the most use and which tend to go neglected. A comfortable seating area with shade gets used almost every day in good weather. A fire pit gets used year after year and becomes the place where families make memories on cool evenings. A well-placed grill or outdoor cooking area gets used regularly if it's convenient to access from the kitchen. A fenced yard with good sightlines from inside the house is used frequently by families with young children.

What tends to go unused? Elaborate water features that require constant maintenance. Expensive outdoor structures built far from the house, which feel disconnected from daily life. Hot tubs that get heavy use the first year and then sit covered for the next five.

The pattern is clear—outdoor features that are simple, accessible, and connected to how your family actually lives get used. Features that require constant upkeep or feel separate from the rest of the home are often forgotten. Invest in what you'll use every week, not what looks impressive on the day it's finished.

For more outdoor living ideas, project inspiration, and guides to help you make the most of your space, visit www.justinskeytohomelife.com.

CHAPTER 20

PERSONALIZING YOUR SPACE

• • •

A HOUSE BECOMES A home through personalization—the choices that make spaces reflect who you are, what you value, where you've been, and how you want to live. This is the difference between a generic nice space and a place that truly feels like yours.

Personalization isn't about spending lots of money or following design rules. It's about making intentional choices that resonate with you, even if others might choose differently. The goal is a home that feels authentic to your life, not a showroom designed to impress strangers.

TELLING YOUR STORY

Your home should tell your story. Not obviously or literally, but through the accumulation of objects, art, and choices that reflect your journey.

Display possessions that have genuine meaning to you. Family photographs that capture important moments and relationships.

Souvenirs from travels that evoke memories of places and experiences. Inherited pieces that connect you to family history. Art that speaks to you personally, whether it's a museum print or your child's painting. Objects you've collected over time that reflect interests and passions.

These personal touches are what make a space feel like home rather than a magazine spread. Interior designers call it a "collected" look versus a "decorated" look—a home that has evolved rather than one assembled all at once according to a predetermined scheme.

Be selective about what you display. Don't show everything you own—curate and rotate. The belongings you display should be ones you actually want to see and think about. Items that no longer resonate can be stored, given away, or let go entirely. Your displayed belongings should reflect who you are now, not who you used to be.

SENTIMENTAL ITEMS AND FAMILY HEIRLOOMS

Some of the most meaningful pieces in a home are the ones you didn't buy for yourself. A piece of furniture from a grandparent. A quilt your mother made. A set of dishes passed down through generations. A framed photograph of someone who shaped who you are. These items carry stories that no store-bought decoration ever will, and they deserve a place in your home even if they don't perfectly match your design scheme.

Not everything has to match. In fact, the homes that feel the most authentic are usually the ones where old and new comfortably sit side by side. A modern sofa next to your grandmother's end table. A contemporary kitchen with a vintage sign on the wall. That imperfect mix is what gives a home character and tells visitors that real people live here with real history. Don't feel pressure to make everything look like it came from the same catalog. The blend is what makes it yours.

COLOR AND PATTERN

Color creates mood and personality. Don't be afraid to move beyond builder beige if neutral doesn't feel like you.

Neutral wall colors do work well as backgrounds, allowing furniture, art, and accessories to stand out. But neutrals don't have to mean boring—there's a wide range of warm whites, soft grays, subtle taupes, and pale colors that provide a neutral backdrop while still having personality.

Introduce more saturated colors through elements that are easier to change than walls. Throw pillows, rugs, curtains, artwork, decorative objects, even the spines of books on shelves—these can add color to a space without a permanent commitment. When your taste evolves, these items can be swapped out more easily than repainting entire rooms.

Pattern adds visual interest but requires balance. One bold pattern in a space creates a focal point. Multiple competing bold patterns create chaos. If you're drawn to pattern, use it thoughtfully—a statement rug, a patterned set of curtains, bold throw pillows—against calmer backgrounds. Mix pattern scales (one large and one small) rather than keep similar, competing scales.

BEYOND WHAT YOU SEE

Personalizing your home goes beyond what you can see. The way a home smells, sounds, and feels under your feet all contribute to how it makes you feel when you walk through the door.

Scent is one of the most powerful triggers for memory and emotion. A candle that reminds you of a place you love, a diffuser with a scent that helps you relax after a long day, fresh flowers on the kitchen table—these small touches shape the experience of being home in ways that paint and furniture alone can't.

Sound matters too. Music playing softly in the background, a water feature on the patio, even the absence of noise in a room designed for quiet—these set the tone for how a space feels.

And texture is what your body actually experiences when you go about your daily routine, walk barefoot, or wrap yourself up in something on the couch. The smooth, cool surface of stone countertops under your hands. A soft rug underfoot in the bathroom on a cold morning. A heavy throw blanket on the sofa for movie nights. These sensory details are what turn a house that looks good into a home that feels good.

COMFORT OVER TRENDS

Design trends come and go. What's stylish this year will look dated in five years. Chasing trends is exhausting, expensive, and ultimately unsatisfying—you're constantly reacting to external standards rather than living according to your own preferences.

Focus instead on what actually makes your life better. Buy furniture that's comfortable to sit on, not just good-looking in photographs. Choose layouts that work for how you actually live, not how design magazines suggest you should live. Prioritize function and comfort, and let style emerge naturally from those practical choices.

Classic pieces age better than trendy ones. A well-made sofa in a neutral color will serve you for decades. An oddly shaped piece in this year's "it" color will look obviously dated within a few years. When investing in major pieces, lean toward timeless rather than trendy.

Save the trendy stuff for easily changeable elements. Accessories, art, textiles—these can follow trends without major commitment. Core pieces should transcend them.

Be especially careful about comparing your home to what you see on social media. Those images are carefully staged, professionally lit, and often sponsored by the brands selling those products. Real homes have clutter, imperfections, and evidence of daily life. That isn't a flaw—that's what makes them real. If scrolling through home design accounts makes you feel like your space isn't good enough, take a step back and remember that you're comparing your everyday reality to someone else's highlight reel. Your home didn't need to look like a photo shoot. It needs to work for your family.

CREATING A REFUGE

Above all, your home should be a place where you feel comfortable, at ease, and able to relax fully. This means different things for different people.

For some, comfort means abundance—layered textures, lots of pillows, soft throws on every surface. For others, comfort means simplicity—clean surfaces, minimal belongings, visual calm. Neither approach is right nor wrong. What matters is aligning your space with what actually makes you feel at peace.

Pay attention to what each space needs. A living room where you entertain might serve your public persona. A bedroom or reading nook serves your need for a private retreat. Not every room needs to make the same statement or meet the same needs.

Lighting plays a huge role in comfort. Harsh overhead lighting makes any room feel sterile and unwelcoming. Layered lighting—a combination of overhead, more focused (task), and ambient sources—lets you adjust the mood to fit the moment. Dimmer switches in living rooms and bedrooms give you control over the atmosphere without changing a single fixture. Even something as simple as turning off the overhead light and turning on a few lamps can transform how a room feels at the end of a long day.

Remember that your home exists to serve your life, not to impress others. Make choices that support how you actually want to live day-to-day. That's the ultimate personalization—a home shaped around your real life rather than someone else's expectations.

ROOMS THAT GROW WITH YOUR FAMILY

Your life isn't static, and your home shouldn't be either. The nursery you design today becomes a toddler's room in two years, a kid's room in five, and a teenager's room after that. A home office might need to double as a guest room when family visits. A playroom eventually becomes a game room or a study space. Think about how each room might evolve as you make design decisions, especially the harder-to-change elements like flooring, built-ins, and wall colors.

Choosing a neutral foundation for rooms that will change purpose makes transitions easier and less expensive. A nursery with soft gray walls and quality hardwood flooring transitions to a teenager's room with nothing more than new bedding, different art on the walls, and updated furniture. A nursery with character-themed wallpaper and bright carpet requires a complete redo when your child outgrows it. Think long-term, invest in the bones, and let the easily changeable elements handle each phase's personality.

SEASONAL TOUCHES

One of the simplest ways to keep your home feeling fresh without spending a lot of money is to rotate small touches with the seasons. Swap throw pillow covers for lighter fabrics and brighter colors in spring and summer, then switch to warmer tones and heavier textures in fall and winter. Change out a wreath on the front door. Rotate the candle scents. Add a bowl of seasonal fruit or a vase of fresh flowers to the kitchen counter. Put out a cozy blanket when the weather turns cool and put it away when the warmth returns.

These small changes keep your home from feeling stale and give you something to look forward to with each new season. They also make your home feel intentional and cared for, which matters both for your own enjoyment and for the impression your home makes on guests. You don't need to redecorate four times a year—just a few small swaps in the rooms you use most can make the whole house feel different.

WHAT MAKES A HOUSE FEEL LIKE HOME

After nearly three decades of walking through homes with families, I can tell you that the ones that feel the best are rarely the most expensive or the most perfectly decorated. They're the ones where you can feel that someone lives there. There are photos on the walls. There's a well-used kitchen with a few things on the counter. There's a favorite chair with a reading light next to it. There's evidence of life within those walls.

The homes that feel cold or empty, even when beautifully finished, look like nobody actually lives in them or would be too afraid to. Everything is too perfect or too staged to be touched or used.

Your home should look like it belongs to you. It should reflect your family, your interests, your history, and the life you're building together. That isn't something you achieve by following a set of design rules. It happens naturally when you stop worrying about what your home is supposed to look like and start making it into the place where your family feels most comfortable and at peace.

• • • RESOURCE • • •

For more design inspiration, seasonal ideas, and resources to help you personalize your space, visit www.justinskeytohomelife.com.

PART FOUR
LIVING YOUR BEST HOME LIFE

CHAPTERS 21–26

OWNING A HOME IS JUST THE BEGINNING.
LIVING WELL IN IT IS THE GOAL.

CHAPTER 21

Smart Home Technology Made Simple

• • •

Technology can make your home more comfortable, efficient, secure, and convenient. But the world of smart-home devices can also be overwhelming—too many options, too much complexity, too much marketing hype, and too little guidance about what actually improves daily life versus what's just expensive novelty.

This is a subject I'm deeply passionate about, and my background in it goes back further than most people would expect. Before my career in building and real estate began, during the same years I was carrying lumber and framing houses for a custom home builder and working for a landscaping company, I started my own networking technology company while I was still in high school. After school, I went out and consulted with businesses, sold, designed, and implemented complete network solutions for them.

Back then, Bayonet Neill–Concelman (BNC) star networks were the norm, and Category 5 (CAT5) networking was just beginning. I converted businesses from that older technology to the new standard and helped them become more efficient. With the old BNC cable networks, if one device on the network went down, a printer, a workstation, anything, the entire network went down with it, and the business would have to immediately pivot to doing everything with pen and paper until someone could get the network back up and running again. I spent a lot of time working with networks, servers, and programming, and I learned early on that technology only matters if it's reliable and actually solves a real problem.

Years later, when smart-home technology started to emerge, I was excited to bring that background into the residential world. I knew it would support my desire to help improve people's home lives. I want to help you think about smart-home technology practically, focusing on what genuinely adds value rather than what looks cool in advertisements.

START WITH PROBLEMS, NOT PRODUCTS

The mistake most people make with smart-home technology is starting with products instead of problems. They see an advertisement or read about a new device and think that seems neat—then buy it without considering whether it actually addresses any need in their life.

Flip that approach. Start with your actual pain points and frustrations, then look for technology that solves them.

Do you constantly worry about whether you locked the door or closed the garage? Smart locks and garage controllers with status notifications can provide peace of mind. Do you come home to a dark house and wish lights were already on? Smart bulbs or switches with scheduling or geofencing can solve that. Do you struggle to maintain comfortable temperatures while keeping energy costs low? A smart thermostat can learn your adjustment patterns and optimize heating and cooling. Do you want to see who's at the door without getting up? A video doorbell provides that capability.

Technology that solves real problems in your daily life gets used. Technology bought on impulse or because it seemed cool often gathers dust after the novelty wears off. Focus your spending on genuine improvements to your daily experience.

Make a list of things that annoy you or cause you stress around the house. Write them down, then research whether technology exists to solve each one. You'll find that some of your biggest frustrations have simple, affordable solutions you didn't know existed. That list becomes your smart-home roadmap, helping you avoid buying products you don't need while making sure you invest in the things that will genuinely improve your life.

CHOOSING AN ECOSYSTEM

Smart-home devices work better when they can communicate with each other. Individual devices doing individual tasks is fine, but the real power comes from automation and integration—lights that turn on when you unlock the door, thermostats that adjust when everyone leaves, cameras that trigger based on other sensors.

To enable this integration, you generally need to choose a primary ecosystem. The major players are Amazon Alexa, Google Home and Assistant, and Apple HomeKit. Each has strengths and limitations; none is objectively best for everyone.

Consider what you already use. If your household is heavily invested in Apple products—iPhones, iPads, Macs, Apple TV—HomeKit integration is seamless and secure. If you use Google services heavily, Google Home makes sense. If you already have

Echo devices or prefer the Alexa voice assistant, the Amazon ecosystem is the natural choice.

You don't have to be exclusive—many devices work with multiple ecosystems—but having a primary platform simplifies setup, control, and automation. Pick one and build around it.

YOUR WI-FI IS THE FOUNDATION

Before you buy a single smart device, make sure your Wi-Fi network can support it. This is the one detail most people overlook, and it's the single most common reason smart-home devices frustrate their owners. A thermostat that loses connection, a doorbell that takes ten seconds to load video, or a lock that didn't respond when you need it—these problems are almost always a Wi-Fi issue, not a device issue.

If your home is larger than a small apartment, a single router in one corner of the house probably won't cut it. Mesh network systems use multiple access points placed throughout the home to provide strong, consistent coverage in every room, including the garage, the basement, and the backyard. They aren't expensive for what they deliver, and they make everything in your smart home work as it should.

In my home, I incorporated Category 6 (CAT6) wiring to support gigabit-speed internet and use three indoor Eero Max 7 mesh network routers along with an outdoor extender. With my networking background, I knew that the physical infrastructure had to be right before anything else would perform the way it should. That same principle I learned decades ago (converting businesses from BNC to CAT5 networking) applies directly to your home today—the network is the foundation on which everything else depends. Get it right first, and everything you add on top of it will work better.

WHERE TO START

If you're new to smart-home technology, certain products offer the best value for most households.

A smart thermostat is often the single best investment. It learns your heating and cooling patterns, adjusts automatically when you're away, provides detailed energy usage data, and typically pays for itself through utility savings within a year or two. Models from ecobee, Nest, and others integrate with most ecosystems and HVAC systems.

Smart lighting provides convenience, energy savings, and security benefits. Start with high-traffic areas—entryways, hallways, living spaces. Scheduling ensures lights are on when you arrive home and off when you leave. Integration with presence sensing means lights respond to you rather than requiring manual switches.

A video doorbell lets you see and communicate with visitors whether you're home, at work, or traveling. You can monitor package deliveries, deter porch pirates, and screen visitors before opening the door. Ring, Nest, and several other brands offer reliable options at various price points.

Smart locks provide keyless entry, the ability to grant temporary access codes for guests or service providers, and logs of who came and went when—no more hiding keys under mats or worrying whether you locked up.

Start with these foundational products, then expand based on what you find useful. Don't buy everything at once—add devices gradually as you learn what works for your household. That's exactly how I did it. When smart-home products first started hitting the market, I began with smart plugs and a first-generation Amazon Alexa. Nothing fancy. I wanted to see how reliable the technology was before I invested further. Once I saw that it worked and genuinely made daily life easier, I added one category at a time, testing each before moving on to the next.

VOICE ASSISTANTS AND ROUTINES

The real power of a smart home isn't controlling one device at a time from your phone. It's automation—setting up routines that chain multiple devices together so your home responds to your life without you having to think about it.

A morning routine might gradually bring the lights up, adjust the thermostat, start your coffee maker, and give you a weather and calendar update—all triggered by a single voice command or automatically at a set time. A bedtime routine might lock the doors, turn off all the lights, arm the security system, and set the thermostat to your sleeping temperature.

A "leaving home" routine might do all of that, plus check that the garage door is closed. These routines take a few minutes to set up and save you time and mental energy every single day. Voice control through a smart speaker also gives you hands-free convenience, especially valuable when you're cooking, carrying groceries, holding a child, or just comfortable on the couch and don't want to get up.

SMART HOME FOR FAMILIES

If you have kids, smart-home technology can make your daily life meaningfully easier. Smart nightlights on schedules provide soft light in hallways and bathrooms without anyone needing to flip a switch in the middle of the night. Baby monitors that integrate with your smart-home system let you check on your child from any screen in the house or on your phone. Intercom features built into smart speakers let you communicate between rooms without shouting across the house—useful for calling kids to dinner, checking on someone in another room, or just avoiding the constant yelling that comes with a busy household.

As kids get older, smart plugs can help manage screen time by controlling when gaming consoles or televisions are powered on. Door sensors let you know when exterior doors open, which matters when you have teenagers coming and going. The goal isn't to turn your home into a surveillance operation—it's to use technology to make parenting a little less stressful and your home a little safer and more organized for the people living in it.

SECURITY AND PRIVACY CONSIDERATIONS

Smart-home devices connect to your network and often to the internet. This creates security and privacy considerations worth taking seriously.

Use strong, unique passwords for all device accounts. Enable two-factor authentication wherever it's offered. Keep device firmware up to date—manufacturers regularly release security patches.

Consider what data devices collect and where it goes. Cameras and microphones inside your home are recording information about your life. Review privacy policies, understand what's stored and shared, and make informed choices about what you're comfortable with. If you have children, this is especially important. Think carefully about where you place cameras and microphones in your home and have honest conversations with your family about what devices are active and why. Smart-home technology should make everyone in the household feel safer and more comfortable, not like they're being monitored.

Consider a separate network for smart-home devices, isolating them from computers and phones that contain sensitive information. Many routers support guest networks that can serve this purpose.

Don't over-automate critical systems without manual backups. A smart lock is great, but keep a physical key accessible. A smart garage opener is convenient, but ensure it can still be operated manually if technology fails.

COMMON MISTAKES AND WHAT I'VE LEARNED

I've set up smart-home technology in my own home and helped countless families think through it in the homes I sell. That process has taught me what works, what doesn't, and where people most often go wrong.

My personal exploratory journey eventually led to something much bigger than my own home. The builder I've represented for the past eight years took the smart-home plan I developed and adopted it as a standard feature in the homes we offer today. But before I could present that plan to my builder, I had to do the homework. I needed to identify the best and most reliable devices and systems that genuinely supported families while still making sense for the builder from a cost perspective. That meant testing products in my own home first, living with them, finding out which ones held up and which ones caused problems, and building a package that I could confidently stand behind. Not everything I tested made the cut. The ones that did are products I recommend because I've used them myself, day in and day out.

The most common mistake I see is buying devices that don't work together. Someone buys a smart lock from one brand, a thermostat from another, lights from a third, and a camera from a fourth—and none of them communicate with each other. You end up with four separate apps on your phone and no ability to create the routines and automations that make smart-home technology actually worth having. Before you buy anything, make sure it works with the ecosystem you've chosen.

The other mistake is overcomplicating things. If your automations are so complex that nobody else in the household can figure them out, you've gone too far. Your family should be able to use the home without needing a tutorial. The best smart-home setups are the ones that work so seamlessly in the background that people barely notice they're there—the lights just come on, the temperature is always comfortable, and the doors lock themselves. That simplicity is what you're aiming for. And always consider what happens when the internet goes down. Every smart device in your home should still function manually. If a power outage or internet disruption leaves your family unable to turn on lights, unlock doors, or adjust the thermostat, the system is too dependent on connectivity.

Today, after years of building and testing one piece at a time, my personal home has smart technology woven into nearly every part of daily life. I have over seven Alexa devices throughout the house, smart lighting inside and outside, smart Christmas lights, a smart thermostat from ecobee, a smart front door deadbolt, a smart garage door opener, AI-powered security cameras, a smart water heater, smart kitchen appliances, a smart washer and dryer, smart irrigation, a smart heat pump, smart floor cleaning robots, and a full alarm system—to name a few. I didn't install all of this at once. It was built gradually over the years, each addition solving a specific problem or improving a specific part of how my family lives. I'm passionate about smart-home technology because I've seen firsthand how much better it makes home life for the people who use it thoughtfully.

SMART HOME AND RESALE VALUE

Buyers increasingly expect smart features in the homes they're considering. A smart thermostat, a video doorbell, smart lighting, and a solid security system all add perceived value, making your home feel modern and move-in ready. These are relatively small investments that signal to buyers that the home has been thoughtfully maintained and updated.

The key is keeping your system simple enough that the next owner can use it without difficulty. If your smart home requires a computer science degree to operate, it's not adding value—it's adding complexity that might actually scare buyers away. Stick with well-known brands, mainstream ecosystems, and straightforward setups. When the time comes to sell, being able to hand a buyer a one-page guide to how the smart home works is a selling point. Handing them a fifty-page manual isn't.

• • • RESOURCE • • •

For smart-home guides, product recommendations, setup tips, and more, visit www.justinskeytohomelife.com.

DEVICE	PURPOSE	COST
SMART THERMOSTAT	SAVE ENERGY, REMOTE CONTROL	$100–$250
VIDEO DOORBELL	SECURITY, PACKAGE MONITORING	$100–$250
SMART LOCK	KEYLESS ENTRY, GUEST CODES	$150–$300
SMART SMOKE DETECTORS	PHONE ALERTS, SELF-TESTING	$100–$150
SMART PLUGS	CONTROL DEVICES REMOTELY	$15–$30 EACH

Table 4: Recommended Smart Home Starter Devices and Costs

•••JUSTIN'S TIP•••

Start with a smart thermostat. It's the single best investment—it pays for itself in energy savings within a year or two, and you'll wonder how you ever lived without being able to adjust the temperature from your phone.

CHAPTER 22
Home Maintenance Made Manageable

• • •

The truth about homeownership that often catches first-time buyers off guard is that owning a home requires constant maintenance. Not occasionally when something breaks, but constantly—month after month, season after season, year after year.

This isn't a flaw in homeownership. It's simply the nature of physical structures. Roofs wear. Paint fades. Systems age. Weather takes its toll. The families who thrive as homeowners are those who accept this reality and build maintenance into their routines rather than fighting it or ignoring it.

Preventive maintenance costs far less—in money, time, and stress—than emergency repairs. A little regular attention keeps small problems from becoming expensive disasters.

CREATING A MAINTENANCE CALENDAR

Breaking maintenance down into manageable seasonal tasks makes the whole process less overwhelming. Instead of a massive list of everything your home needs, you have focused checklists appropriate to each time of year.

Spring maintenance focuses on recovering from winter and preparing for warmer months. Service your air conditioning before you need it—a tune-up catches problems before the first hot day. Clean gutters of winter debris that may have accumulated. Inspect the roof and exterior for any damage from winter weather. Check caulking around windows and doors, refreshing where it's cracked or missing. Service or sharpen lawn equipment before mowing season. Test your irrigation system, if you have one, to check for leaks and adjust heads.

Summer maintenance includes ongoing lawn and garden care, as well as checking weatherstripping and sealing around doors and windows while it's easy to work outside. Clean the dryer vent regularly and thoroughly—lint buildup is a fire hazard. Touch up exterior paint where needed. Service any outdoor equipment you use regularly.

Fall is about preparing for winter. Have your heating system serviced before cold weather arrives. Clean gutters of leaves—this is critical to prevent ice dams and water damage. If you have a fireplace or wood stove, have the chimney inspected and cleaned. Make sure to winterize irrigation systems and outdoor faucets in cold climates. Check weatherstripping and add insulation where needed. Test smoke and carbon monoxide detectors, and replace batteries.

Winter maintenance is lighter but not absent. Monitor for ice dams if you're in a cold climate. Keep walkways and driveways clear for safety. Change HVAC filters monthly during heating season. Periodically check that nothing is showing signs of freezing or winter damage.

THE COST OF IGNORING MAINTENANCE

Every item on that seasonal calendar exists because skipping them leads to something worse. A gutter cleaning that costs a couple of hundred dollars, if skipped, can lead to water backing up under your roof or overflowing against your foundation—and then you're looking at thousands in water damage repair. An HVAC tune-up that costs around $150 keeps your system running efficiently and catches small issues before they become catastrophic failures that require a full replacement costing several thousand dollars or more. Caulking around windows and doors costs almost nothing. It takes an afternoon, but ignoring this step allows moisture to seep into your walls, where it can cause mold, rot, and structural damage that's extremely expensive to remediate.

The pattern is always the same. Small, affordable, routine maintenance gets skipped because it doesn't feel urgent. Then the problem grows quietly behind the scenes until it becomes an emergency that costs five, ten, or twenty times what the preventive step would have cost. I've seen this play out over and over in nearly three decades of working with homeowners. Families who stay on top of their maintenance spend less on their homes over time than those who ignore it until something breaks.

THE 1 PERCENT RULE

A common guideline is to budget roughly 1 percent of your home value annually for maintenance and repairs. A $350,000 home needs about $3,500 per year—roughly $290 per month—for upkeep.

Some years you'll spend much less than this, handling only minor maintenance and no major repairs. Other years, when the HVAC fails or the roof needs replacement, you'll spend much more. The average works out over time.

The key is building this fund before you need it. Treat your maintenance savings like any other fixed expense—automatically transfer them to a dedicated account on a regular schedule. When something breaks, the money is there. You handle it calmly rather than scrambling for credit or deferring repairs that will only get worse.

Older homes and homes with aging systems may need more than 1 percent. Newer homes typically need less in the early years, but you should still build a fund for eventual needs.

KNOW WHAT YOU OWN AND HOW LONG IT LASTS

Every major system and appliance in your home has a general life expectancy, and knowing those numbers helps you plan ahead of time rather than being caught off guard. A typical asphalt shingle roof lasts about twenty to twenty-five years. An HVAC system usually lasts fifteen to twenty years with proper maintenance. Water heaters last about ten to fifteen years. Dishwashers, refrigerators, and washers and dryers generally last ten to fifteen years, depending on the brand and how heavily they're used. Garage door openers typically last ten to fifteen years.

These are averages, not guarantees. Some systems last longer with excellent care, and some fail earlier due to manufacturing issues, heavy use, or neglect. The point isn't to predict the exact year something will break but to have a general sense of when major expenses are coming. If your water heater is twelve years old, it's not a crisis yet, but it's time to start researching replacements and budgeting for one. If your roof is approaching twenty years old, get it inspected annually and start setting money aside. Being ahead of these timelines turns a potential emergency into a planned expense, and that's a much more comfortable way to own a home.

DIY VS. PROFESSIONAL HELP

Some maintenance tasks are appropriate for most homeowners: changing HVAC filters, cleaning gutters if you can safely reach them, basic caulking and weatherstripping, minor paint touch-ups, simple fixture replacements, and basic landscaping tasks.

Other tasks should generally be left to professionals: electrical work beyond changing fixtures; anything involving gas lines or gas appliances; roof repairs (safety risk); HVAC system repair (complexity and refrigerant handling); structural modifications; and anything requiring permits.

Between these extremes is a gray area that depends on your skills, comfort level, available time, and the specific situation. Be honest with yourself. YouTube makes everything look easy, but reality is often messier. The cost of professional help is usually less than the cost of fixing amateur mistakes, and far less than the cost of injuries from tasks beyond your competence. When in doubt, hire it out.

KEEP A HOME MAINTENANCE LOG

One of the best habits you can develop as a homeowner is keeping a maintenance log. This doesn't need to be complicated. A simple notebook, a spreadsheet, or even a notes app on your phone will work. Every time you have maintenance performed or DIY, write down what was done, the date, who did the work, and what it cost—record when major systems were installed or replaced. Keep receipts and warranty information in one place.

This log becomes invaluable in several ways. It tells you when something is due for service again—you won't have to guess whether the HVAC was serviced six months ago or eighteen months ago. It provides documentation if a warranty claim ever arises. And when the time comes to sell your home, a well-maintained log is one of the most reassuring things you can hand a potential buyer. It shows them that the home has been cared for, that systems have been maintained on schedule, and that there's a clear history of everything that has been done. Buyers notice this, and it builds the kind of confidence that helps a sale go smoothly.

BUILDING PROFESSIONAL RELATIONSHIPS

Before you need them urgently, identify and establish relationships with professionals for various home needs: a plumber, an electrician, an HVAC technician, a reliable handyman, a roofer, and an arborist for tree service.

Get recommendations from neighbors and friends. Consider having them out for minor work to evaluate their responsiveness, quality, and pricing before you're in an emergency. It's much better to have a trusted plumber's number in your contacts before your water heater fails than to be desperately searching during a crisis.

Keep a short list of your go-to professionals somewhere accessible—in your phone, on the refrigerator, wherever you'll actually look when something goes wrong. Include their name, phone number, and what they do. When the furnace stops working on a freezing night or a pipe bursts on a weekend, you don't want to be reading online reviews and comparing quotes. You want to call someone you already trust and know will show up.

Building relationships with good tradespeople means they'll prioritize you when you call. Being a regular customer who pays promptly and treats them well has value when you need help quickly.

HOME WARRANTIES

Home warranties are service contracts that cover the repair or replacement of major systems and appliances for a set period, usually one year, in exchange for an annual premium and a service fee each time you file a claim. They're common in resale transactions where the seller or buyer's agent includes one as part of the deal, and some new-construction builders offer them as well.

There are some common misconceptions about home warranties worth understanding. They don't cover everything—most have exclusions for preexisting conditions, improper maintenance, and cosmetic issues. They typically let the warranty company choose the contractor, which means you may not get the professional you'd have selected yourself. And the coverage limits on individual items can sometimes be lower than the actual cost of replacement.

That said, for some homeowners—especially first-time buyers or those purchasing older homes with aging systems—a home warranty can provide peace of mind and protection against unexpected major expenses during the first year of ownership. Read the contract carefully, understand what is and isn't covered, and weigh the cost of the premium against the age and condition of your home's systems before deciding whether it makes sense for you.

WHAT I'VE SEEN OVER THE YEARS

After nearly three decades in this industry, I can tell you that the difference between a home that holds its value and one that doesn't almost always comes down to maintenance. I've walked through homes that are fifteen or twenty years old and look almost new because the owners stayed on top of everything. I've walked through homes half that age that look tired and worn because maintenance was deferred year after year.

The difference is most pronounced at resale. A well-maintained home inspects better, appraises better, and sells faster. Buyers can feel it when they walk through a home that has been cared for—the systems work quietly, the finishes are clean, and there's a sense that the home has been respected. On the other hand, deferred maintenance shows up in home inspections as a long list of items that need attention, and that list scares buyers, leads to renegotiations, and can cost the seller far more than the maintenance would have cost in the first place. Taking care of your home isn't just about comfort while you live there. It's one of the smartest financial decisions you can make as a homeowner.

• • • RESOURCE • • •

For seasonal maintenance checklists, planning tools, and more resources to help you stay on top of your home, visit www.justinskeytohomelife.com.

• • • KEY TAKEAWAY • • •

Budget approximately 1 percent of your home's value per year for maintenance and repairs. A $300,000 home means setting aside $3,000 annually—or $250 per month. Some years you'll spend less; some years you'll spend more. The reserve keeps you ready.

CHAPTER 23

Energy Efficiency and Sustainability

• • •

Energy-efficient homes are more comfortable to live in, less expensive to operate, and better for the environment. Whether your primary motivation is saving money, reducing environmental impact, or simply enjoying a more comfortable home—or some combination of all three—improving your home energy performance makes sense.

The good news is that efficiency improvements exist at every budget level, from free behavioral changes to significant investments with substantial paybacks.

UNDERSTANDING YOUR ENERGY USE

Before spending money on improvements, understand where your energy currently goes. This knowledge helps you prioritize efforts toward the biggest impacts.

Your utility services may offer free or subsidized home energy audits. Auditors examine insulation levels, air sealing, window performance, HVAC efficiency, and other factors, then provide prioritized recommendations. This expert assessment is often the best starting point.

Even without a formal audit, you can learn a lot by examining your utility bills. Look at usage patterns across seasons. How much does heating or cooling increase your bill compared to mild months? How has usage trended over the years? Are there anomalies that suggest problems?

In a typical home, heating and cooling account for 40 to 52 percent of energy use. Water heating adds another 15 to 20 percent. Appliances, lighting, and electronics make up the rest. The biggest opportunities for savings are usually in the biggest categories.

IT'S NOT JUST ABOUT SAVING MONEY

Most conversations about energy efficiency focus on utility bills, and the savings are real. But the benefit that people underestimate the most is comfort. A well-insulated, properly sealed home feels different from a drafty one. Temperatures stay more consistent from room to room. You don't have hot spots and cold spots depending on where you're standing. Drafts near windows and exterior walls disappear. Outside noise is noticeably reduced. Humidity is easier to control in both summer and winter.

These aren't small differences. Living in a tight, well-insulated home is genuinely more pleasant than living in a leaky one. Once you've experienced it, you notice it immediately when you walk into a home that hasn't been upgraded. If the only reason you're considering energy efficiency improvements is to lower your utility bill, you're missing the bigger picture. The comfort alone is worth the investment.

LOW-COST AND NO-COST IMPROVEMENTS

Many efficiency gains require little or no investment—just attention and changed habits.

Air sealing is one of the most cost-effective improvements you can make. Sealing gaps and cracks around windows, doors, pipes, wires, and other penetrations reduces drafts and energy loss. Weatherstripping, caulk, and spray foam cost little and can make a noticeable difference in comfort and efficiency.

Replacing incandescent bulbs with LEDs reduces lighting energy use by 75 to 80 percent while bulbs last fifteen to twenty-five times longer. If you haven't completed this switch throughout your home, it's one of the simplest wins you can make.

Programming your thermostat appropriately—or better yet, installing a smart thermostat that learns and adjusts automatically—reduces heating and cooling when you're asleep or away without sacrificing comfort when you're home. Lowering the temperature by 7 to 10 degrees for eight hours a day can save 10 percent or more on heating and cooling costs.

Insulating hot water pipes, especially the first several feet from the water heater, reduces heat loss and can let you lower the water heater temperature setting. Speaking of which, 120 degrees Fahrenheit (49 degrees Celsius) is adequate for most households and safer than higher settings because it greatly reduces a scalding safety hazard.

Using cold water for laundry saves the energy that would otherwise be used to heat water—a significant amount for households with frequent laundry loads.

Running ceiling fans lets you raise the thermostat setting by several degrees while maintaining comfort. Moving air feels cooler than still air, so fans let you use less air conditioning without feeling warmer. In the winter, reverse the direction of your ceiling fans to push warm air that has risen to the ceiling back down into the living space. Most ceiling fans have a small switch on the motor housing that changes the rotation direction. It's a free improvement that many homeowners don't know about.

None of these low-cost improvements requires a contractor or a large budget. They're the kind of changes you can do over a weekend, and the cumulative effect of doing all of them is often more significant than any single expensive upgrade. Start here before spending money on bigger projects.

LARGER INVESTMENTS

Beyond the basics, more significant investments offer substantial returns.

Adding insulation, particularly in under-insulated attics, can significantly reduce heating and cooling costs. Many older homes have insulation levels well below current recommendations. The payback period for insulation upgrades is typically reasonable, and the comfort improvements are immediate.

Replace single-pane or failing double-pane windows with modern high-efficiency windows that reduce heat transfer and may also reduce noise. The investment is substantial, but comfort and energy savings make it worthwhile, particularly if existing windows are in poor condition. If replacing all the windows at once isn't in your budget, prioritize the ones on the sides of the house that get the most sun exposure or the ones in rooms where you notice the most drafts. Even replacing a few at a time makes a difference.

Heat pump water heaters use a fraction of the energy of conventional electric water heaters—typically two to three times less. If your electric water heater is approaching the end of its life, a heat pump replacement can provide significant ongoing savings.

Solar panels can reduce or eliminate electricity costs, and with declining installation costs and available incentives, the economics have become attractive in many regions. Get multiple quotes, understand the realistic production estimates for your specific situation, and factor in available tax credits and incentives.

HEATING AND COOLING IS YOUR BIGGEST LEVER

Since heating and cooling represent the single largest portion of your energy use, your HVAC system deserves special attention. If you're replacing an aging system, understand your options.

A traditional combination of a furnace and air conditioning is what most people know. However, heat pump technology has advanced significantly and now offers both heating and cooling in a single system with much higher efficiency. Modern heat pumps can operate effectively in cold climates that would have been a problem for older models.

Look at Seasonal Energy Efficiency Ratio (SEER) ratings for cooling efficiency and Heating Seasonal Performance Factor (HSPF) ratings for heating efficiency—higher numbers mean better performance. And make sure your system is properly sized for your home. An oversized system cycles on and off too frequently, wasting energy and wearing out faster. An undersized system runs constantly and never quite keeps up. A qualified HVAC professional should perform a load calculation specific to your home rather than just matching the size of the old unit.

Don't overlook your ductwork. Even the most efficient system in the world wastes energy if conditioned air is leaking out through gaps, disconnections, or poorly sealed joints in your ducts before it ever reaches the rooms it's meant to heat or cool. Having your ductwork inspected and sealed can improve the performance of your existing system without replacing anything.

A couple of years ago, I upgraded my home and replaced my old heat pump furnace with a geothermal heat pump system. I was able to take advantage of local tax incentives to help offset the cost. However, even with those incentives, it was still significantly more expensive upfront than replacing it with a standard midgrade heat pump would have been.

After living with it, would I do it again? Yes—but differently. If I could do it over, I'd have focused on updating my insulation, windows, and doors first. Even with this amazing system, it's still limited by how tight your home is and how well the building envelope keeps heat in during winter and air conditioning in during summer.

My old furnace had to be replaced at the time, so I decided to go ahead with the geothermal, knowing I'd need to address the other items later. The good news is that a geothermal system lasts significantly longer than a conventional heat pump, so the long-term value is there. But the lesson I learned is an important one—the best HVAC system in the world can only do so much if the home around it isn't properly sealed and insulated. Start with the envelope, then upgrade the system. If your situation forces you to do it in the other order as mine did, know that the full benefit comes when both pieces are in place.

TAX CREDITS AND INCENTIVES

In the US, federal tax credits, state programs, and local utility rebates can significantly offset the cost of energy efficiency upgrades. The Inflation Reduction Act expanded federal tax credits for a wide range of home improvements, including heat pumps, insulation, windows and doors, water heaters, and electrical panel upgrades. These credits can cover a meaningful percentage of the cost and are available annually up to certain limits, which means you can spread larger projects across multiple tax years to maximize the benefit.

Many state and local utility companies offer their own rebate programs in addition to federal credits. Some utilities offer free or discounted energy audits, rebates on insulation and air sealing, and incentives for upgrading to high-efficiency appliances. These programs change frequently, so check with your utility provider and your state energy office to find out what's currently available in your area. The combined savings from federal credits, state programs, and utility rebates can reduce the effective cost of major upgrades by 30 percent or more, dramatically changing the math on whether an improvement makes financial sense for your family.

NEW CONSTRUCTION VS. EXISTING HOMES

From my perspective, working on both sides of the industry, one of the biggest advantages of buying a new-construction home is that energy efficiency is built in from the start. Current building codes require significantly better insulation, air sealing, window performance, and HVAC efficiency than what was standard even ten or fifteen years ago. The builder I represent goes beyond code minimums with high-efficiency systems, better insulation packages, and tighter construction as standard features—not upgrades. When you buy new, you get the benefit of modern building science without having to retrofit anything.

If you're buying an existing home, that doesn't mean you're out of luck—it just means your efficiency improvements will come in stages. Start with the items that give you the most return for the least cost: air sealing, attic insulation, and a smart thermostat. Then work your way toward bigger projects, such as windows, doors, and HVAC upgrades, as your budget and timeline allow. The key is having a plan and working through it over time rather than trying to do everything at once or ignoring it entirely.

Evaluate any significant investment based on your specific situation, local energy costs, available incentives, and how long you plan to stay in the home. What makes sense varies considerably based on these factors. But regardless of your budget, improving your home's energy efficiency is one of the few upgrades that pays you back every single month through lower utility bills while simultaneously making your home more comfortable to live in.

•••RESOURCE•••

For energy efficiency guides, information on current incentives, and more resources to help you make smart upgrades, visit www.justinskeytohomelife.com.

IMPROVEMENT	COST	PAYBACK
LED LIGHT BULBS	$50–$100	<1 YEAR
SMART THERMOSTAT	$100–$250	1–2 YEARS
AIR SEALING	$100–$300	1–2 YEARS
ATTIC INSULATION	$1,000–$2,500	4–8 YEARS
SOLAR PANELS	$15,000–$30,000	8–15 YEARS

Table 5: Energy Efficiency Upgrades, Costs, and Payback Periods

•••JUSTIN'S TIP•••

Start with the cheap modifications: LED bulbs, weatherstripping, and a smart thermostat. These have the fastest payback. Then work your way up to bigger investments like insulation. The expensive upgrades—windows, solar, geothermal—make sense if you plan to stay long-term.

CHAPTER 24

Home Safety and Security

Your home should be a safe haven—a place where you and your family are protected from hazards and threats. A few straightforward precautions and preparations can significantly reduce risks to both your loved ones and your property.

Safety and security are related but distinct concerns. Safety focuses on protecting you and your loved ones from accidents and hazards within the home—fires, falls, and carbon monoxide. Security focuses on protecting against external threats—break-ins, theft, unwanted intrusion. A well-protected home addresses both.

FIRE SAFETY

Fire kills more people in homes than any other type of disaster. Fortunately, most fire deaths are preventable with basic precautions.

Smoke detectors are the most important fire safety measure. Install detectors on every level of your home, in each bedroom, and outside sleeping areas. Test them monthly by pressing the test button. Replace batteries at least annually—many people do this when clocks change in spring or fall. And replace the detector units themselves every ten years, as sensors degrade over time.

Fire extinguishers should be accessible in the kitchen, garage, and any workshop areas. Learn how to use them before you need to. Remember to pull the pin, aim at the base of the fire, squeeze the handle, and sweep side to side (PASS). But also remember that extinguishers are for small fires—if a fire is growing, get out and call 911.

Have a family escape plan. Every member of your household should know two ways out of every room and where to meet outside. Practice the plan so the response is automatic—there's no time for planning during an actual fire. Make sure windows can be opened easily and that any security bars have quick-release mechanisms.

Carbon monoxide (CO) detectors are equally critical. This colorless, odorless gas can be fatal before you even realize there's a problem. Install CO detectors near bedrooms and on every level of the home. If the alarm sounds, get everyone outside immediately and call 911.

CHILDPROOFING AND EVERYDAY FAMILY SAFETY

If you have young children, your home needs to be safe from more than fire and break-ins. Everyday hazards that adults barely notice can pose serious risks to toddlers and small children. Outlet covers on every unused outlet, cabinet locks on anything containing cleaning products or sharp objects, and stair gates at the top and bottom of staircases are the basics most parents know. But others get overlooked.

Secure heavy furniture, such as dressers, bookshelves, and televisions, to the wall with anti-tip brackets. Children climb, and unsecured furniture can topple with devastating consequences. This takes minutes to install and costs almost nothing.

If you have a pool or hot tub, make sure it's surrounded by a self-closing, self-latching fence that meets local code requirements. Drowning is one of the leading causes of accidental death for young children, and barriers are the most effective prevention.

Keep garage hazards in mind, too—tools, chemicals, and heavy equipment should be stored up high or behind locked cabinets. As a father, I can tell you that your perspective on home safety changes completely the moment you have a child. You start seeing hazards everywhere you never noticed before. The good news is that most of them are easy and inexpensive to address once you're aware of them.

HOME SECURITY BASICS

Most burglars are opportunists who take the easiest target. Basic security measures make your home less attractive, sending them elsewhere.

Solid exterior doors with quality deadbolts are your first line of defense. Deadbolts should have at least a one-inch throw (the distance it protrudes) and be installed in reinforced door frames—the frame is often the weak point when doors are forced. Consider upgrading strike plates on the door jamb with longer screws that reach the wall studs.

Sliding glass doors are particularly vulnerable. Install a security bar or pin that prevents them from being forced open, even if the lock is defeated. Secondary locks specifically designed for sliders add protection.

Ground-floor windows, especially those hidden from street view, are common entry points. Ensure all windows have working locks. Consider window sensors as part of an alarm system. Reinforce glass with break-resistant film on particularly vulnerable windows.

Lighting deters intruders who prefer to work in darkness. Motion-activated lights around entry points and dark areas of your property make approaches more visible. Interior lights on timers or smart controls make your home look occupied when you're away.

Landscaping can help or hurt security. Trim bushes near windows and doors so they don't provide hiding spots. Thorny plants under ground-floor windows discourage that route. Keep trees trimmed to prevent approaches to second-floor access points.

PROTECTING AGAINST WATER DAMAGE

Water damage is one of the most common and most expensive home insurance claims, and much of it is preventable. Know where your main water shutoff valve is before you ever need it in an emergency. If a pipe bursts or a supply line fails, being able to shut off the water in seconds rather than minutes can be the difference between a small cleanup and a devastating flood.

Check the supply hoses on your washing machine and dishwasher periodically. Rubber hoses degrade over time and are a common source of leaks. Replace them with braided stainless-steel hoses, which are far more durable and resistant to bursting. If you have a basement, a sump pump with a battery backup is essential in areas prone to heavy rain or high water tables—the primary pump keeps water out during normal storms, and the battery backup takes over during power outages when you need it most.

Smart water leak sensors placed near water heaters, washing machines, sinks, and sump pumps can alert you to leaks immediately via your phone, giving you time to act before minor drips turn into major damage. A smart water shutoff valve takes this a step further by automatically shutting off the water supply when a leak is detected, even if you're not home.

TECHNOLOGY FOR SECURITY

Modern security technology offers capabilities that were expensive and complicated just a decade ago.

Video doorbells let you see and communicate with anyone at your door from anywhere with your smartphone. You can verify visitors, accept deliveries, and deter suspicious activity without being home.

Security cameras have become affordable and easy to install. Wireless battery-powered cameras can be placed almost anywhere without running wires. Cloud storage preserves footage even if cameras are damaged. Visible cameras deter some intruders, while others provide evidence in the event of an incident.

Smart locks eliminate the need for hidden keys while providing access logs and the ability to grant temporary codes to guests, service providers, or trusted neighbors. You can verify whether doors are locked from anywhere and lock them remotely if needed.

Monitored security systems provide a professional response to alarms. When sensors are triggered, the monitoring company contacts you and can dispatch emergency services if needed. This adds ongoing monthly costs but provides peace of mind and a verified response.

I mentioned earlier in this book that my home was broken into before I renovated it. When the police crime lab came out and dusted for fingerprints, one of the first things they asked was whether I had cameras. I didn't, and we never found out who did it. That experience changed everything about how I approach home security.

It doesn't matter how safe your neighborhood is supposed to be—crime happens everywhere, and the feeling of having your home violated stays with you. Since then, I've installed cameras outside and inside certain areas of my home, along with a full alarm system, smart locks, and smart lighting. Again, my family jokes that I've turned into Jason Bourne, but the peace of mind is real. I'd rather have these systems and never need them than need them and not have them.

YOUR NEIGHBORS ARE YOUR BEST SECURITY SYSTEM

No technology replaces having neighbors who look out for each other. Get to know the people who live around you and exchange phone numbers. Let them know when you'll be traveling and ask them to keep an eye on things. Offer to do the same for them. A neighbor who notices an unfamiliar vehicle in your driveway or a package sitting on your porch for too long is often more effective than any camera, because a neighbor can act on what they see in real time.

Community watch programs, neighborhood social media groups, and even casual relationships with the people on your street create a network of awareness that makes the entire neighborhood safer. This costs nothing and is one of the most effective security measures available to any homeowner.

INSURANCE AND DOCUMENTATION

Even with the best safety and security measures in place, things can still go wrong. Your insurance policy is your financial safety net, and it deserves more attention than most homeowners give it. Review your coverage annually to ensure it reflects the current replacement cost of your home and belongings. Many homeowners are underinsured because their policy hasn't kept pace with rising construction costs or because they've made improvements that were never reported to their insurer.

Do a home inventory. Walk through every room and take photos or videos of your belongings, including items in closets, cabinets, and other storage areas. Keep a list of high-value items, including estimated values and any receipts or appraisals. Store this documentation in a cloud storage account, a safe deposit box, or with a trusted family member outside your home. If a fire, flood, or theft ever occurs, this inventory is what allows you to file a complete and accurate insurance claim. Without it, you're relying on memory during one of the most stressful moments of your life, and you'll inevitably forget things. This takes an afternoon to do and should be updated whenever you make significant purchases or changes to your home.

• • • RESOURCE • • •

For home safety checklists, security planning guides, and more resources to help protect your family and your investment, visit www.justinskeytohomelife.com.

EMERGENCY PREPAREDNESS

Beyond ongoing safety and security, be prepared for emergencies—such as natural disasters, extended power outages, and other disruptions.

Know where your utility shutoffs are: the water main, the gas valve (if applicable), and the electrical main. In certain emergencies, quickly shutting these off can prevent further damage or danger.

Keep basic emergency supplies accessible: flashlights and batteries, a battery-powered radio, a first-aid kit, basic medications, bottled water, and non-perishable food sufficient for at least three days. Store important documents in a waterproof container that can be grabbed quickly in an emergency or during an evacuation.

If you live in an area prone to power outages from storms, ice, or high winds, consider investing in a portable or whole-house generator. A portable generator can keep your refrigerator, sump pump, and a few essential circuits running during an outage. A whole-house generator connected to your electrical panel turns on automatically when power is lost and keeps everything running until the grid is restored. Either option provides significant peace of mind during severe weather.

Know the specific weather risks in your area—whether that's hurricanes, tornadoes, flooding, ice storms, or extreme heat—and prepare for the scenarios that are most likely to affect your home.

Have a communication plan, so family members can connect and confirm safety if normal channels are disrupted. Preparation reduces panic when unexpected events occur, allowing you to respond effectively rather than scrambling.

CHAPTER 25
Building Community

• • •

A house is where you sleep. A neighborhood is where you live. The community around your home affects your daily experience, your sense of belonging, and your quality of life as much as anything within your four walls.

Homeownership often anchors people to places in ways that renting does not. You're not just passing through; you've made an investment and a commitment. This stability creates an opportunity to build genuine connections with neighbors and become part of something larger than your household.

GETTING TO KNOW YOUR NEIGHBORS

The simplest form of community building starts with getting to know people nearby. This doesn't require becoming best friends—just establishing the basic familiarity that makes a neighborhood feel like a neighborhood rather than a collection of strangers who happen to live near each other.

Introduce yourself when you move in. Walk around with cookies or a friendly note. A simple, "Hi, we just moved in next door," breaks the ice and starts the relationship.

A wave as you come and go, a brief chat while getting the mail or doing yard work, a friendly hello when paths cross—these small interactions build familiarity over time. You don't need lengthy conversations. You only need enough contact that neighbors aren't strangers to you.

Once you're settled, consider hosting a simple gathering. It doesn't need to be elaborate. It can be having drinks on the patio, a cookout, or even just coffee and pastries on a Saturday morning. The invitation itself signals openness to connection. Many people want community but are too shy or busy to initiate. Being the one who makes the first move helps everyone open up a bit.

THE UNIQUE OPPORTUNITY OF NEW CONSTRUCTION

If you're buying in a new-construction community, you have a unique opportunity that people moving into established neighborhoods don't. When everyone is moving in around the same time, no "established" neighbor has been there for decades, and no newcomer feels like an outsider. Everyone is starting fresh together. Everyone is finding their way at the same time. That shared experience creates a natural bond and makes it easier to form connections than in a neighborhood where social patterns are already established.

I've seen this happen over and over in the communities where I sell homes. Families who close on their home purchases within weeks of each other become lifelong friends. Kids who grew up together in these neighborhoods stay connected even after they've moved away. The early days of a new community, when construction is still happening, and everyone is landscaping their yards and figuring out where to put the trash cans, are actually some of the best times to form those connections. Take advantage of it. Be one of the people who reach out, who introduce themselves, who suggest a neighborhood gathering before the community is even finished being built. Those early relationships often become the foundation of a tight-knit neighborhood for years to come.

CONTRIBUTING TO YOUR COMMUNITY

Good neighbors contribute positively to their neighborhoods by maintaining their own property and engaging with the broader community.

Property maintenance matters beyond your own satisfaction. The appearance of your home affects your neighbors and the whole neighborhood. Unkempt yards, peeling paint, and accumulated junk detract from others' enjoyment and can affect property values. Keeping your property well-maintained is part of being a good neighbor.

Participate in neighborhood activities when they exist, such as block parties, garage sales, holiday events, neighborhood watch programs, and community cleanups. If they don't exist, consider starting something. It doesn't have to be elaborate. A simple annual tradition like a summer cookout or a holiday cookie exchange can become something neighbors look forward to year after year. Even small traditions, once established, create connection and give people a reason to talk to each other.

Look out for neighbors, especially those who might be vulnerable—elderly residents living alone, families with new babies, anyone going through difficult times. Collecting mail when others travel, keeping an eye on a neighbor's property, helping with occasional tasks, checking in during extreme weather—these small kindnesses build real relationships.

If you have a homeowners association, participate rather than just complaining. Attend meetings. Maybe serve on the board or a committee. Decisions are made by those who show up. If you want input on how your community is run, you have to engage.

BE THE NEIGHBOR YOU WANT TO HAVE

Most neighbor friction comes from small things that accumulate over time. Being thoughtful about a few basics goes a long way toward preventing problems and building goodwill.

Be mindful of noise. Loud music, barking dogs, late-night gatherings, and early morning lawn equipment all affect the people around you. You don't have to live in silence, but being aware of timing and volume shows respect for your neighbors' peace. Park considerately—don't block driveways, take up multiple street spots, or make it difficult for others to navigate the neighborhood. If you have pets, keep them under control and clean up after them. Nothing sours a neighbor relationship faster than repeatedly finding or stepping on dog poop left on their lawn.

If you're planning a project that might affect your neighbors, such as construction, tree removal, a new fence, or a large gathering, give them a heads-up beforehand. They may not have any objection, but they'll appreciate being informed rather than surprised. And if you need to borrow something, return it promptly and in the same condition you received it. These are small courtesies, but they're the foundation of being someone people are glad to live next to.

FINDING YOUR PEOPLE

Beyond immediate neighbors, homeownership presents the opportunity to put down roots and build broader community connections.

Local organizations aligned with your interests, such as book clubs, gardening groups, sports leagues, faith communities, service clubs, and hobby groups, provide ready-made communities of people with something in common. The shared interest gives you something to talk about, and the regular interaction builds relationships over time.

Volunteering connects you with like-minded people while contributing to your broader community. Schools, libraries, food banks, youth programs, environmental groups, animal shelters—whatever causes you care about—there are probably local organizations doing that work who'd welcome help.

Local businesses appreciate regular customers and often become community hubs. The coffee shop where the owner knows your order. The hardware store where the staff remembers what projects you're working on. The restaurant where the staff greets you by name. These relationships add texture to daily life and make you feel like you belong somewhere specific rather than just occupying space in a generic town.

The important part is being intentional. Community rarely happens by accident for adults the way it sometimes does for children. You have to put yourself in situations where relationships can form, show up consistently, and be open to connecting with people who are different from you. It takes time—months or even years—for acquaintances to become friends and for a neighborhood to feel like home. But the investment pays dividends for as long as you live there.

Community didn't happen automatically. It requires effort, openness, and time. But the reward—a sense of belonging, mutual support, shared life—is one of the great gifts of settled homeownership.

KIDS AS COMMUNITY CONNECTORS

If you have children, your community experience will be shaped significantly by them. Kids are natural community connectors in ways that adults often aren't. They meet other kids at the bus stop, on the playground, at school, and on sports teams, and those connections naturally lead to connections between parents. You end up meeting people you might never have talked to otherwise because your kids became friends first.

School involvement—volunteering in classrooms, attending events, joining the parent-teacher association (PTA)—puts you in regular contact with other parents from your area. Youth sports leagues do the same thing, with the bonus of spending hours on the sidelines together, where conversation happens naturally.

As a father, I've found that some of the strongest community connections I've made have come through my son. Parents bonding over shared experiences with their children creates a specific kind of friendship that's hard to replicate any other way. If you have kids and are looking for community, lean into the opportunities that parenting naturally creates.

WHEN COMMUNITY IS HARD

I want to acknowledge that not everyone lands in a naturally friendly neighborhood, and not everyone has the time, energy, or personality for deep community engagement. Life circumstances vary. Work schedules, health challenges, family demands, and simple introversion all affect how much capacity someone has for building relationships outside their household. That's okay.

Start small if that's what you can manage. Even knowing one or two neighbors well enough to exchange phone numbers and keep an eye on each other's homes makes a difference. You don't need to be friends with everyone on your street. And remember that community doesn't have to come from your immediate neighborhood. It can come from your workplace, your church, your gym, your kids' school, or any other place where you spend time with the same people regularly. The goal is simply to have people in your life beyond your household who you can rely on and who can rely on you. Where you find those people matters less than finding them.

WHAT COMMUNITY HAS MEANT TO ME

As a father, a community has meant more to me than I can easily put into words. Let me give you an example. Recently, on a windy day, our two amazing Labrador retrievers got out because the gate blew open. My wife called me, and I was an hour away at work. It was one of the most stressful moments because our dogs aren't just dogs to us—they're family.

I immediately called my neighbor across the street, and they and another neighbor set out into the neighborhood right away. They went far behind our house into another community, and a woman asked them if they were looking for dogs. She asked for a description and realized she knew where they were. That lady and her husband had found our dogs and put them safely in their fenced backyard. My neighbor loaded them into his truck and brought them back to our house. They were lifesavers.

I made sure to go to my neighbors and the family who found our dogs to thank them and give them gifts of appreciation. None of them wanted to accept anything. They said, "That's what neighbors are for." What great people. That's community. That's what it means to have people around you who show up when it matters.

Raising a family isn't meant to be done in isolation, and neither is maintaining a home or building a life. The neighbors who wave when we pull into the driveway, the friends who show up when things get hard, the families whose kids play with our son—these relationships are part of what makes our house feel like a home.

Homeownership gives you the stability to invest in relationships that take time to build. Unlike renting, where you might move every year or two, owning a home anchors you to a place long enough for real connections to form. That stability is a gift. Use it. The walls and roof keep you sheltered, but the people around you are what make it a life worth living.

CHAPTER 26

The Rhythms of Home Life

• • •

Owning a home isn't just about having a building. It's about the life that happens inside it: the daily rhythms, the seasonal patterns, the accumulated moments that transform a house into your home.

This chapter isn't about specific tasks or skills. It's about stepping back and thinking about the life you're creating within your walls—how your home serves you, how you move through it, how it supports the person you want to be and the family you want to build.

CREATING SPACES THAT SERVE YOU

Think about how each space in your home supports—or didn't support—your daily life.

Morning routines set the tone for the day. Does your bathroom configuration align with your household's wake-up patterns, or does it create conflict and stress? Is the kitchen set up to support how you actually make breakfast, whether that's elaborate cooking or grabbing something quick? Is there a place to put keys, wallet, bag, and other essentials when leaving, or do you waste time searching for them every morning? A smooth morning makes everything that follows feel more manageable. A chaotic morning leaves everyone frazzled before the day has even really begun. Small changes to how your home is organized can make a significant difference in how your family starts each day.

Evening wind-down matters for wellbeing. Where does your family naturally gather? Is that space comfortable and conducive to relaxation? Can work be put away so evenings feel separate from daytime responsibilities? Is there a place for quiet decompression and a place for family interaction?

Weekend rhythms differ from weekday ones. Where do hobbies happen? Where does meal prep for the week ahead happen? Where do kids play when they have more time? Where do you recharge and restore yourself?

Adjust spaces to support how you actually live, not how you think you should live or how previous residents configured things. Furniture can move. Rooms can serve different purposes than their names suggest. Your home should work for your real life.

Pay attention to the friction points in your daily life at home. If the same problem frustrates you every day—the coat closet that's too small, the kitchen counter that's always cluttered, the entryway where shoes pile up—those are signals that something needs to change. Sometimes the fix is simple: a hook on the wall, a basket by the door, a different furniture arrangement. Other times, it requires more thought or investment. But the goal is always the same: reduce daily friction so that living in your home feels easy rather than a constant battle with your own space.

THE SEASONS OF HOME AND FAMILY

Your home will serve you differently as your family grows and changes. The house that works perfectly for newlyweds needs to adapt when children arrive. The home set up for toddlers will need to shift when those children become teenagers. Eventually, if you stay long enough, the house that was bursting with activity becomes quiet again as kids move out and start their own lives.

This isn't a problem to solve. It's the natural rhythm of life, and your home adapts with you. The playroom becomes a study. The nursery becomes a guest room. The formal dining room you never used becomes the homework station you use every day. Part of living well in your home is being willing to let it evolve as your needs evolve, rather than clinging to how things were set up when you first moved in. The home that serves you well is the one that grows with you through every season.

ESTABLISHING ROUTINES

Homeownership rewards routine. Maintenance done consistently stays manageable; deferred, it snowballs into overwhelming projects. Finances tracked regularly stay healthy; ignored, they drift toward trouble. Spaces maintained daily stay pleasant; neglected, they become sources of stress.

Build home care into your regular schedule. Weekly cleaning prevents deep cleaning emergencies. Monthly checks catch small problems early. Seasonal tasks done on schedule prevent crises.

The specific days and times matter less than the consistency. Maybe Saturday mornings are when the bathrooms get cleaned. Maybe the first weekend of each month is when you walk the property looking for issues. Maybe the start of each season triggers a checklist of tasks. Find what works for your schedule and stick to it. When home maintenance becomes routine, it stops feeling like a burden and becomes just another part of how you live.

Financial routines keep homeownership sustainable. Regular budget reviews. Consistent contributions to maintenance and improvement funds. Periodic reviews of insurance coverage, utility costs, and property tax assessments. When these financial rhythms become automatic, you stop worrying about whether you can afford the next repair or whether you're falling behind on the costs of homeownership. The discipline of regular attention prevents the anxiety of neglect.

Family routines create stability and memory. Regular meal times when possible. Consistent bedtimes for children. Weekly family activities that everyone can count on. These rhythms create the fabric of family life. Children especially thrive on predictability. Knowing what to expect—that Sunday mornings mean pancakes, that Friday nights mean pizza and a movie, that bedtime follows the same comforting sequence—gives them a sense of security that carries into every other part of their lives.

TRADITIONS AND RITUALS

Beyond daily routines, the traditions and rituals you establish in your home become part of your family's identity. These are the things your children will remember long after they grow up and move away. The way you celebrate birthdays. The holiday traditions that are unique to your family. Sunday dinners. Movie nights. The special breakfast you make on the first day of school. The way you decorate for each season. The songs you sing, the games you play, the stories you tell.

These traditions don't have to be elaborate or expensive. Some of the most meaningful ones are the simplest. What matters is the consistency and the intention behind them. Maybe it's the way you always read one more book at bedtime, even when you're tired. Maybe it's the Saturday morning trip to the farmers market or the annual camping trip to the same spot every summer. Maybe it's the way birthdays always start with breakfast in bed or the way snow days mean hot chocolate and board games. These small, repeated moments add up to something much larger over time.

When your children grow up and start their own families, they'll carry these traditions forward, adapted for their own lives but rooted in what they experienced in your home. That's how a house becomes more than a building. It becomes the place where your family's story is written.

MAKING ROOM FOR REST

Your home should be a place of restoration, not just another source of demands.

Create spaces for quiet, even if just a corner with a comfortable chair where you can sit undisturbed. Everyone needs somewhere to decompress. This matters for every member of the household. Parents need a place to reset after long days. Children need spaces where they can calm down and be alone with their thoughts. Even in a small home, carving out a quiet corner or establishing quiet times can make a significant difference in how your family experiences daily life.

Protect some time from productivity. Not every hour at home needs to be spent accomplishing something. Rest, leisure, play, simply being—these have value too. In a culture that constantly tells us to optimize and hustle, it can feel almost rebellious to simply sit on your porch and watch the evening settle in, or to spend a Saturday afternoon doing absolutely nothing of consequence. But these moments matter. They're when you actually experience your home rather than just using it as a base of operations between activities.

Let your home be a refuge from the world's demands, not an extension of them. The endless to-do list will always have more items. Learning to be at peace in your home, even with imperfection, is part of actually living there rather than just maintaining it.

TECHNOLOGY AND BOUNDARIES

One of the greatest challenges to home life today is the way technology blurs every boundary. Work emails follow you to the dinner table. Social media competes for attention during family time. Screens can fill every quiet moment if you let them. Your home should have spaces and times that are protected from the constant pull of devices.

Consider establishing technology-free zones or times. No phones at the dinner table. No screens in bedrooms after a certain hour. Designated times when devices get put away, and the family is fully present with each other. These boundaries aren't about being anti-technology—technology has its place and its benefits, as I've discussed throughout this book. But home life requires presence, and presence requires boundaries. The memories your family makes won't come from everyone sitting in the same room staring at their own screens. They'll come from the moments when you're truly together.

WHEN RHYTHMS GET DISRUPTED

Life throws curveballs. Illness, job changes, new babies, losses, unexpected crises—these moments disrupt even the most carefully established routines. Your home rhythms will sometimes fall apart. That's not a failure. That's life. There will be seasons when dinner is takeout more often than not, when the laundry piles up, when the bedtime routine gets compressed or skipped entirely. There will be times when survival mode is the only mode available, and the carefully built rhythms have to wait.

The goal isn't to maintain perfect routines through chaos. The goal is to have a foundation you can return to when the disruption passes. The routines and traditions you establish during stable times become anchors that help your family find its way back to normal after difficult seasons. When things fall apart temporarily, don't waste energy feeling guilty about it. Focus on getting through the hard time, and trust that the rhythms you've built will be there waiting for you on the other side.

FINDING YOUR FAMILY'S RHYTHMS

Every family's rhythms are different. What works for your neighbors may not work for you, and that's perfectly fine. The goal isn't to copy someone else's routines or live up to some idealized picture of home life. The goal is to pay attention to what actually works for your family—what brings you together, what gives you energy, what makes your house feel like home—and build more of that.

In our home, we've learned this through experience. The rhythms we've established—the way mornings work, the traditions we look forward to, the places where we gather as a family—these developed over time, through trial and error, through adjusting what wasn't working and leaning into what was. Your home will find its own rhythms, too. Be patient with the process, be willing to experiment, and don't be afraid to change things that aren't serving your family well. The rhythms you establish will become the heartbeat of your home life.

PART FIVE
BUILDING YOUR FUTURE

CHAPTERS 27–30

WHAT YOU BUILD TODAY BECOMES
YOUR FAMILY LEGACY TOMORROW.

CHAPTER 27

Building Equity and Wealth

• • •

Your home is more than a place to live. It's an asset—potentially the most valuable one you'll ever own. Understanding how to build and leverage home equity is part of using homeownership strategically to improve your long-term financial position.

This chapter is about thinking of your home not just as a shelter, but as a wealth-building tool that, managed well, can provide financial security and opportunity for decades to come.

HOW EQUITY GROWS

Home equity is simply the difference between what your home is worth and what you still owe on it. If your home is worth $350,000 and you owe $280,000 on your mortgage, you have $70,000 in equity. Equity grows in two ways: paying down your mortgage and appreciation in your home value.

Every mortgage payment includes some principal reduction—a portion that actually reduces your loan balance rather than just paying interest. In the early years of a mortgage, most of each payment goes to interest, and only a small amount reduces principal. Over time, as the balance decreases, the split shifts and more goes to principal. This automatic equity building, month after month, year after year, is one of the significant advantages of owning over renting.

Appreciation—increase in your home market value—builds equity without any payment from you. Historically, home values have increased, though not uniformly across markets or periods. Some areas appreciate faster than others. Some periods see rapid gains while others see stagnation or even decline. Over long time horizons, appreciation has generally been positive, but it's not guaranteed.

These two forces working together mean that homeowners typically build substantial equity over time—equity that renters, no matter how long they pay rent, never accumulate.

THE POWER OF FORCED SAVINGS

One of the most underappreciated benefits of homeownership is that it forces you to build wealth, whether you're thinking about it or not. Every month, when you make your mortgage payment, part of that payment reduces your loan balance and increases your equity. It happens automatically. You don't have to decide to save that money. You don't have to exercise willpower or discipline. The structure of homeownership does the work for you.

For people who struggle to save money—and that includes a lot of us—this forced savings mechanism is incredibly powerful. A renter who intends to save the difference between renting and owning often doesn't follow through. Life happens, expenses come up, and the money gets spent on other things. But a homeowner who makes their mortgage payment every month is building equity, regardless of what else is happening in their financial life. Over ten, twenty, or thirty years, this automatic wealth-building adds up to a substantial asset that wouldn't exist otherwise.

WHAT THE NUMBERS LOOK LIKE OVER TIME

To make this concrete, consider a family that buys a home for $400,000 with a 10 percent down payment of $40,000. They take out a thirty-year mortgage at 7 percent for the remaining $360,000. Their starting equity is $40,000—their down payment.

After ten years of making regular payments, they've paid down about $50,000 in principal. If the home has appreciated at a modest 3 percent annually, it's now worth roughly $537,000. Their equity has grown from $40,000 to approximately $227,000—the increase in home value minus the remaining loan balance. After twenty years, assuming continued modest appreciation, that equity could be over $400,000. And if they stay until the mortgage is paid off in thirty years, they own the home outright, with equity equal to the property's full market value.

These are illustrations, not predictions. Your actual numbers will depend on your purchase price, loan terms, and how the market performs in your area. But the general principle holds: homeownership builds wealth over time in ways that renting can't match. A renter who pays the same amount in rent for thirty years ends up with nothing to show for it except receipts. A homeowner who pays the same amount in mortgage payments ends up owning a valuable asset free and clear. That difference is one of the most significant financial distinctions in American life.

ACCELERATING EQUITY BUILDING

While equity builds automatically through normal mortgage payments and market appreciation, you can accelerate the process with intentional strategies.

Extra principal payments go directly toward reducing your loan balance, and the numbers are striking. If you make just one extra full mortgage payment per year applied directly to principal, you can cut a thirty-year mortgage down to roughly twenty-four years—saving about six years of payments. If you can manage two extra full payments per year, you can pay off that same thirty-year mortgage in approximately twenty years, saving a full decade of payments and a substantial amount of interest over the life of the loan.

I usually recommend that first-time buyers go with a thirty-year mortgage rather than a shorter term. The lower monthly payment gives you room to breathe—you can still live your life, handle unexpected expenses, and not feel house poor. But I encourage them to aim for one to two extra full principal payments each year when they can.

The key point is that when something major happens in life—a job loss, a medical emergency, a car that needs replacing—you can redirect that money toward the emergency and still maintain your regular mortgage payment without stress. You have flexibility built in. If you had locked yourself into a fifteen-year mortgage with a higher required payment, you wouldn't have that cushion when you need it most.

Bi-weekly payment programs—making half your monthly payment every two weeks instead of one full payment monthly—result in twenty-six half-payments per year, which equals thirteen full payments instead of twelve. This accelerates payoff without it feeling like a major sacrifice.

Refinancing to a shorter term—going from a thirty-year mortgage to a fifteen-year one, for example—means higher monthly payments but dramatically faster equity building and much less total interest paid over the life of the loan. This makes sense when the higher payment fits comfortably in your budget.

None of these accelerations is required or even always wise. If you have higher-interest debt, paying that off first usually makes more sense. If you need the cash flow flexibility, lower payments might be the right choice. Evaluate acceleration strategies against your complete financial picture.

WHEN PAYING DOWN YOUR MORTGAGE FASTER ISN'T THE BEST MOVE

It's worth being explicit about when accelerating your mortgage payoff isn't the smartest financial move. If you have credit card debt or other high-interest debt, pay that off first. The interest rate on credit cards is almost certainly higher than your mortgage rate, so every dollar you put toward credit card debt saves you more than a dollar toward your mortgage.

If you don't have an adequate emergency fund, build that first. Life is unpredictable, and having three to six months of expenses in savings protects you from taking on new debt when something goes wrong. Extra mortgage payments are great, but not if they leave you vulnerable to the next car repair or medical bill.

I know firsthand how devastating it can be to face a crisis without savings. Years ago, my Mother, my sister, and I had just moved to the Alabama coast and were struggling to get established when the BP oil spill happened. It was horrible. There was no way to earn a living—everything stopped. It took the BP claims process a very long time to start making payments. Because we had been struggling just to get established, we had not been able to build any emergency fund. Worse, because we had not been residents of Alabama long enough, we couldn't get any assistance from the state. Churches and nonprofits were completely wiped out of resources. We were in a void with no help anywhere.

I had some credit cards, so we maxed them out merely to eat. We waived almost every bill just to survive. This was one of the times my credit was destroyed. I remember my Mother crying, holding one egg and a box of tuna helper, saying, "This is the only food we have."

Then, thanks to God, the husband of a married couple I had worked with and become friends with showed up at the place we were renting to say hello and check on us. They were in the same boat as us, but they had been in the area for a long time. He and I stood outside and made small talk, asking how each other was doing. I didn't tell him what we were going through.

When we said goodbye, we shook hands, and I felt something. I looked down and saw a bundle of cash. I told him I couldn't take it. He said yes, I could. He said he knew we needed it—although we had told no one our actual financial position. He said I could pay him back one day when I was able, even if it was years from now. Then he told me something that has stuck with me ever since: "When we help people with a genuine heart, God rewards us tenfold."

Since that moment, I've tried to pay it forward—to help people I come across who are in need, not to get a reward or favor, but because of what that family did for us. They literally saved us. I'm not trying to make this book about my spiritual beliefs. I share this story to show you how bad it can get without emergency savings. Build your emergency fund before you worry about paying down your mortgage faster. You never know when life will throw something at you that you couldn't have predicted.

If your employer offers a 401 (k) match and you're not contributing enough to get the full match, that's essentially free money you're leaving on the table. A 50 percent or 100 percent match on your contributions beats almost any other return you could get, including paying down your mortgage. Get the full match before accelerating mortgage payments.

STRATEGIC HOME IMPROVEMENTS

Some home improvements build equity by increasing your home value more than they cost. We discussed this in detail in Part Three: kitchen and bathroom updates, curb appeal improvements, and adding usable space often returns more than its investment.

Improvements that add measurable value actively build equity. Improvements that merely maintain the home prevent equity erosion. Improvements that are highly personalized or over-improve for the neighborhood may cost more than they add.

Think of strategic improvements as another form of equity investment—putting money into your property and getting increased value in return. Maintenance also matters for equity. Deferred maintenance erodes value. A home that shows obvious neglect sells for less than one that has been well cared for. Protecting your equity means maintaining your property, not just making improvements.

YOUR HOME IN YOUR OVERALL FINANCIAL PICTURE

Your home is likely to be a significant part of your net worth, but it shouldn't be the only part. Diversification matters in personal finance just as it does in investing. Having all your wealth tied up in a single asset—even a valuable one like your home—creates risk. Home values can decline. Local markets can stagnate. Life circumstances can force a sale at an inopportune time.

A healthy financial picture includes home equity alongside retirement accounts, emergency savings, and possibly other investments. Don't pour every available dollar into your house at the expense of funding your 401 (k), building your emergency fund, or saving for other goals. Your home is one piece of a larger puzzle, and the pieces should work together to provide both security now and options later.

LEVERAGING HOME EQUITY

As equity builds, it becomes a financial resource you can potentially access.

Home equity loans and home equity lines of credit (HELOCs) allow you to borrow against your equity, typically at interest rates lower than credit cards or personal loans. This borrowed money can fund home improvements, education expenses, debt consolidation, or other significant needs.

But borrowing against equity carries real risks. Your home secures the loan. If you can't repay, you could lose your home. People who borrow against equity for consumption rather than investment often regret it—they've turned their home into an ATM and reduced the wealth they've built.

I've seen families tap their equity repeatedly over the years, always with good reasons at the time, and end up with almost no equity left after decades of homeownership. They have a house, but not the wealth that should have come with it. On the other hand, I've seen families who treated their home equity as untouchable except for true emergencies or investments that would generate returns, and they ended up with a substantial financial cushion that gave them real options later in life.

Use home equity strategically, not casually. Borrowing to improve the home itself often makes sense. Borrowing for investments in education or business might make sense. Borrowing for vacations or everyday consumption rarely does.

When you eventually sell your home, your equity is what you walk away with after paying off the remaining mortgage and selling costs. This can fund a down payment on your next home, provide retirement income, or help you achieve other financial goals. Building equity is building options for your future self.

WHAT I'VE SEEN OVER THE YEARS

In nearly three decades of working in this industry, I've seen homeownership build substantial wealth for countless families. I've seen first-time buyers who stretched to afford their home and then, fifteen or twenty years later, found themselves sitting on hundreds of thousands of dollars in equity. I've seen families use that equity to fund their children's education, start businesses, retire comfortably, or pass something meaningful to the next generation.

The key is thinking long-term. Homeownership builds wealth slowly, steadily, and sometimes almost invisibly. The families who benefit most are the ones who buy a home they can afford, maintain it well, stay long enough for equity to build, and resist the temptation to treat their home like an ATM along the way. It isn't glamorous, and it doesn't happen overnight. But over the course of a lifetime, homeownership remains one of the most accessible and reliable paths to building real wealth for ordinary families.

•••RESOURCE•••

For equity calculators, financial planning tools, and more resources to help you build wealth through homeownership, visit www.justinskeytohomelife.com.

YEAR	HOME VALUE	MORTGAGE BALANCE	YOUR EQUITY
0 (PURCHASE)	$400,000	$360,000	$40,000
10	$537,600	$310,200	$227,400
20	$722,400	$221,800	$500,600
30	$970,900	$0	$970,900

Table 6: How Home Equity Grows Over 30 Years

•••JUSTIN'S TIP•••

Go with a thirty-year mortgage for the lower payment, but aim to make one to two extra payments to principal each year when you can. This gives you flexibility. If an emergency hits, you can redirect that money. You're not locked into the higher payment of a fifteen-year loan, but you still pay it off early.

CHAPTER 28
When to Consider Moving

• • •

Most people don't stay in their first home forever. Lives change. Families grow or shrink. Jobs relocate. Needs evolve. The home that was perfect when you bought it may no longer fit a decade later.

Knowing when to stay and when to move is part of the ongoing homeownership journey. Moving is expensive and disruptive, but staying in a home that no longer serves you has costs, too.

SIGNS IT MIGHT BE TIME TO MOVE

You have outgrown the space. The home that fit perfectly when you bought it no longer works for your family size or needs. Children have arrived or grown. You need a home office space that didn't exist. Storage is maxed out. Bathrooms are bottlenecked every morning. The dining room has become a homework station, and there's nowhere left for actual dining. Adding on might be possible, but it isn't always practical or cost-effective compared to finding a different home. Before you commit to moving, though, make sure you have honestly evaluated all the possibilities in your current space—sometimes creative reconfiguration can solve problems you thought required more square footage.

Your commute has become unbearable. Job changes have significantly increased your drive time, and the hours lost to commuting are affecting your quality of life, family time, and energy levels. A ninety-minute commute each way is three hours of your day, fifteen hours of your week, spent in a car instead of with your family or doing things that matter to you. The costs in time, stress, and missed moments might outweigh the benefits of staying put, and remote work has changed the equation for some families. However, if your job requires you to be there in person, where you live relative to where you work matters enormously.

The neighborhood has changed in ways that no longer suit you. For better or worse, neighborhoods evolve. What was right when you moved in might no longer be right. Schools may have changed. Traffic patterns may have shifted. Development may have altered the character. Demographics may have evolved in ways that affect your sense of belonging.

Maintenance is overwhelming. Older homes require more attention. If the upkeep burden exceeds what you can reasonably handle—physically, financially, or just in terms of time and mental energy—a newer or smaller home might make more sense. This is especially relevant as you age. The house that was manageable in your forties might feel like a full-time job in your sixties or seventies. A large yard, multiple levels, and aging systems all demand attention. There's no shame in admitting that a home has become more than you want to manage and finding something that fits your current capacity and lifestyle.

Your life stage has shifted. Empty nesters often want to downsize. Retirees might want single-level living, a different climate, or proximity to healthcare. Changing physical needs might require accessibility features your current home lacks. Life stages bring different requirements.

FINANCIAL CONSIDERATIONS

Moving costs money—significant money. Understanding the full financial picture helps you decide whether moving makes sense.

Selling costs include agent commissions, closing costs, and potential repairs or updates needed to sell. With the changes from the NAR settlement discussed earlier in this book, commission structures may be negotiated differently than in the past, but there are still costs involved on both sides of the transaction. When you add in closing costs and the work often needed to prepare a home for sale, expect total selling costs of 8 to 10 percent of your sale price. On a $350,000 home, that's $28,000 to $35,000 in costs just to sell.

Buying costs include closing costs on your new home, moving expenses, and the inevitable purchases and updates that come with any new place. Budget another few percentage points of the new home price.

Consider whether improvements might address your needs more economically than moving. A bathroom addition, a basement finishing, a kitchen renovation, or a master suite expansion might give you the functionality you need for less than the combined costs of selling, buying, and moving. This is especially worth considering if you have a favorable interest rate locked in.

Spending $50,000 on a major renovation that lets you stay in a home with a 3 percent mortgage may make more financial sense than selling, buying, and taking on a new mortgage at 7 percent—even if the new home would have been perfect without needing any work.

Interest rates matter significantly. If you have a great rate locked in from when rates were lower, moving means financing at current rates, which might be significantly higher. This is a reality many homeowners face right now. If you bought or refinanced when rates were in the 3 percent range, and current rates are in the 6 or 7 percent range, moving to a similarly priced home could add hundreds of dollars to your monthly payment. On a $350,000 mortgage, the difference between a 3 percent rate and a 7 percent rate is roughly $700 per month—over $8,000 per year. That's real money that affects your quality of life and your ability to save for other goals. Some families who'd otherwise move are choosing to stay and renovate specifically because giving up their low rate didn't make financial sense.

Your equity position also affects your options. If you have substantial equity built up, you have flexibility—that equity can serve as your down payment on your next home and help offset moving costs. If you're underwater or barely above water on your mortgage, moving may not be feasible at all without bringing money to the closing table. Before you start seriously considering a move, know where you stand. Get a realistic estimate of what your home would sell for and compare it to what you owe. That number tells you what you actually have to work with.

Run the numbers carefully. Sometimes moving makes clear financial sense. Other times, the costs mean staying and adapting is the better choice.

IMPROVE OR MOVE

Before deciding to move, honestly evaluate whether improvements to your current home could address your needs. Some problems can be solved with renovation. You need more space? A home addition, a finished basement, or a converted attic might provide it. Do the kitchen or bathrooms feel dated? Renovation can transform them. Need a home office? A spare-room conversion or a garage build-out might work.

Other problems can't be solved with renovation. You can't renovate away a bad commute. You can't add bedrooms if your lot is too small and zoning doesn't allow it. You can't change the school district. You can't fix a neighborhood that no longer feels safe or welcoming. You can't add a backyard if you don't have one. These are the issues that genuinely require moving to solve.

Compare the cost of renovating to the cost of moving. Get real estimates for the improvements you'd need to make your current home work, and compare that to the total cost of selling, buying, and moving. Sometimes the answer is obvious. Sometimes it's close, and other factors, like the interest rate environment or your emotional attachment to the home, will tip the balance.

DON'T TRY TO TIME THE MARKET

People often ask me whether they should wait to sell because prices might go up, or rush to buy before prices rise further, or hold off if they think the market is about to drop. My answer is almost always the same: don't make major life decisions based on where you think the real estate market is heading, because nobody can reliably predict what prices or interest rates will do.

If you need to move because of a job, a growing family, or a life change, do so when you need to. If your current home no longer serves you, address that when it becomes a real problem, not based on predictions about what the market will do six months or two years from now. I've seen people delay moves, waiting for the perfect moment, only to watch conditions change in ways they didn't expect. I've seen people rush into decisions they weren't ready for because they feared missing out. Make decisions based on your life circumstances, your financial readiness, and your family's needs—not based on speculation about the market.

EMOTIONAL FACTORS

Beyond finances, emotional factors deserve consideration.

Your home holds memories. The door frame where you marked the kids' heights. The kitchen where holiday meals were prepared. The yard where birthday parties happened. The bedroom where babies slept. These have value that spreadsheets can't capture.

But staying somewhere that no longer serves you also has emotional costs. The frustration of a too-small space. The time lost to excessive commuting. The stress of maintenance that never ends. The feeling of being stuck rather than settled. The low-grade daily irritation of living in a home that fights against your life instead of supporting it. These costs don't show up on a spreadsheet, but they're real, and over the years, they add up to something significant.

Neither pure finance nor pure sentiment should drive the decision alone. Weigh both honestly. Consider what matters most to you and your family. Make a decision you can live with, knowing there's rarely a perfect answer.

WHAT I'VE LEARNED HELPING FAMILIES DECIDE

In nearly three decades of working with families on both sides of this decision, I've seen people move too soon and regret it. They underestimated the costs, overestimated how much better the next place would be, or simply didn't give their current home a fair chance. I've also seen people stay too long and regret it—years spent frustrated in a home that no longer fit, waiting for a perfect moment that never came, or putting off a move until health or circumstances made it much harder than it needed to be.

My advice is to be honest with yourself about what isn't working and why. If the problems are fixable with renovation, seriously consider that path—especially if you have a low interest rate you don't want to give up. If the problems are about location, commute, schools, or fundamental space limitations that can't be addressed, then moving is probably the right answer. Don't let fear of change keep you stuck somewhere that's making your life harder than it needs to be. And don't let restlessness or the appeal of something new push you into a move you aren't financially or emotionally ready for.

• • • RESOURCE • • •

For moving cost calculators, comparison tools, and more resources to help you think through this decision, visit www.justinskeytohomelife.com.

• • • KEY TAKEAWAY • • •

Don't try to time the market. No one can reliably predict where prices or rates are going. Make your decision based on your life circumstances, your financial readiness, and your family needs—not speculation. People who wait for the perfect moment often watch it pass them by.

CHAPTER 29
Leaving a Legacy

• • •

For many families, homeownership is about more than one generation. It's about building something that benefits those who come after—creating stability, wealth, and opportunity that extends beyond your own lifetime.

This chapter is about the longer view: what homeownership can mean for your family legacy and how to think about passing along both tangible assets and intangible values.

BREAKING CYCLES AND BUILDING NEW ONES

For some families, homeownership represents breaking a cycle. Maybe you grew up in instability—moving from apartment to apartment, never having a place that was truly yours, watching your parents struggle with landlords, evictions, or the uncertainty of not knowing where you'd be living next year. When you buy a home, you're not just buying a building. You're saying that the cycle stops here. Your children will have stability. They'll have roots. They'll have something you didn't have.

For other families, homeownership is a continuation of a tradition. Your parents owned their home, and their parents before them. The expectation was always that you'd do the same, and you're passing that expectation along to your children. Either way—whether you're the first in your family to own or the latest in a long line—what you do matters. The patterns you establish, the stability you create, and the values you model will ripple forward into generations you may never meet.

TEACHING FINANCIAL LESSONS

Your children are watching everything you do, including how you handle money and maintain your home. The lessons they absorb—spoken and unspoken—will shape their own financial futures.

Let them see the work of homeownership. Explain why you're saving for repairs, how the mortgage works, what maintenance you're doing, and why. Demystify the financial side so they understand homeownership as achievable and manageable rather than mysterious and overwhelming.

Involve them appropriately as they grow. Age-appropriate chores teach responsibility for shared space. Including them in decisions helps them understand how choices get made. Explaining trade-offs helps them grasp that resources are finite and must be allocated thoughtfully.

Model good financial behavior. Children learn more from what they observe than from what they're told. How you handle money, how you make decisions, how you balance spending and saving—these patterns become templates for their own lives.

Talk explicitly about money when appropriate. Many families avoid discussing finances, treating money as taboo. But children who grow up without understanding how money works are at a disadvantage when they face financial decisions as adults. You don't need to share every detail of your financial situation, but helping them understand concepts like budgeting, saving, debt, and how mortgages work prepares them for their own financial lives. Age-appropriate financial education is one of the most valuable gifts you can give your children—it costs nothing and pays dividends for the rest of their lives.

CREATING FAMILY WEALTH

Homeownership has been a primary wealth-building vehicle for generations of American families. The stability, the forced savings through mortgage payments, the appreciation over time—these factors combine to build assets that can be passed forward.

Home equity can help the next generation in various ways. It might fund college education, providing the opportunity to start their adult lives without crushing student debt. It might provide help with their first down payment, giving them a head start on their own homeownership journey. It might serve as an emergency backup when they face unexpected challenges. Or it might provide for your own retirement so that your needs don't become a financial burden on your children when you're older. The equity you build isn't just yours—it has the potential to change the trajectory of your family for generations.

Estate planning ensures your assets go where you intend. How your home is titled, what happens to it when you pass, how to minimize tax implications, and whether a trust makes sense—these are questions to discuss with qualified legal and financial advisors. Proper planning can preserve wealth that poor planning would erode.

But wealth transfer isn't just about the house itself. The financial habits and knowledge you model and teach may be more valuable than the dollars you leave behind. Teaching children to manage money wisely, to save consistently, to make thoughtful decisions—these skills compound over their lifetimes.

PRACTICAL WAYS TO HELP THE NEXT GENERATION

Beyond leaving equity when you pass, there are practical ways to help your children or grandchildren get started on their own homeownership journey. You can teach them to save for a down payment while they're still young, helping them open savings accounts and understand the power of consistency over time. You can help them understand how credit works—how to build it, how to protect it, why it matters when they're ready to buy.

If you're in a position to help financially, you might provide gift funds toward their down payment—there are specific rules and documentation requirements for this that their lender will explain. You might let adult children live at home for a period while they save aggressively for their own place. You might co-sign a loan, though this carries real risk and should be done with a full understanding of what you're taking on. The goal isn't to create dependency but to give them a foundation from which to build their own financial independence.

HAVING THE CONVERSATION ABOUT THE HOUSE

One of the most valuable things you can do for your family is have honest conversations about what happens to your home when you're gone. Too many families avoid this topic until it's too late, and then adult children are left making difficult decisions while grieving, often with different assumptions about what should happen.

Do your adult children want to keep the house? Can they afford to? Does one child want it while another needs the cash from a sale? Is it better to sell and divide the proceeds? These conversations can be uncomfortable, but they prevent conflict later. Make your wishes clear, put them in writing with proper legal documentation, and give your family the gift of knowing what you want rather than having to guess.

THE MEMORY FACTOR

Beyond money, homes hold memories that form family identity.

The house where the grandparents lived. The kitchen where special recipes were made. The porch where stories were told. The backyard where generations played. The bedroom where children slept, dreamed, and grew up. The dining room table at which holidays were celebrated year after year. These places become part of the family narrative, anchoring memories and connecting past to present. When your children are grown, they'll remember not just the house itself but everything that happened inside it.

Creating a home full of good memories is its own kind of legacy. The stability you provide, the traditions you establish, the experiences you share—these shape who your children become and what they remember when they're grown. They'll remember the feeling of coming home, of knowing they had a place that was theirs, of being surrounded by people who loved them. That feeling of security and belonging will influence how they create their own homes and raise their own families.

Not every home needs to stay in the family forever. The memories don't require keeping the physical structure. But recognizing that your home is where your family's story is being written gives weight to how you live there day-to-day.

You're creating memories right now that your children will carry for the rest of their lives. That's a legacy worth being intentional about.

LEGACY BEYOND YOUR FAMILY

Legacy isn't only about what you leave to your own children. It's also about what you contribute to the broader community and how you model generosity for the next generation. Our family supports the Friends of Finn Foundation, a nonprofit that provides comfort items to pediatric cancer and bone marrow transplant patients during treatment. The foundation was started by my nephew Finn himself—a twelve-year-old boy who, while fighting his own courageous battle with cancer, wanted to help other kids going through the same thing he was. After Finn passed away, his parents, my chosen brother, and his wife continued the work he had started. They formed the foundation, honoring his memory by helping the families and children he had cared so deeply about.

Finn's legacy isn't a house or money. It's the lives he touched, the comfort he brought to other children in their darkest moments, and the inspiration he left behind for everyone who knew him. A twelve-year-old boy showed all of us what it means to think of others, even when you're suffering yourself. That's the kind of legacy that matters—the kind that changes lives and ripples outward in ways you can't measure.

Your legacy might look different. Maybe it's volunteering in your community, serving on a local board, mentoring young people, or simply being the neighbor who shows up when someone needs help. Remember the story I told earlier in this book about the man who handed me a bundle of cash when my family had nothing, who told me that when we help people with a genuine heart, God rewards us tenfold? That moment changed my life. It changed how I see my responsibility to others. The legacy he left in my life had nothing to do with a house or money. It was about showing me what it means to help someone when they need it most.

WHAT MY MOTHER GAVE ME

I started this book by telling you about my Mother—how she raised me as a single parent, how she worked multiple jobs, how she gave me everything she could, even when she had almost nothing. She never owned a home. She couldn't leave me property, equity, or a down payment for my first house.

What she left me was something more valuable. She gave me resilience. She gave me a work ethic. She gave me the belief that things could be better, that I could build a different life, that struggle didn't have to be the end of the story. She gave me values that guided me through the hardest times and helped me build everything I have today. That's legacy. Not every parent can pass on a house. But every parent can pass on something that matters.

If you're in a position to leave your children a home, equity, and financial stability, that's a tremendous gift. But never forget that the intangible legacy—the values, the memories, the example you set—may matter even more. Your children are watching. They're learning from everything you do. The way you handle adversity, the way you treat others, the way you show up for your family day after day—that's the legacy they'll carry forward, whether or not they ever inherit a single dollar.

CHAPTER 30

Your Ongoing Journey

• • •

We've covered a lot of ground together in these pages—from the fundamentals of financial preparation through the home-buying process, to making your house a home, living well within it, and building toward the future.

But turning the last page of this book isn't an ending. It's a beginning. Homeownership is a journey that continues long after closing day, evolving as your life unfolds, presenting new challenges and opportunities at every stage. I've poured nearly three decades of experience into these pages—everything I've learned from helping families navigate this journey, from my own struggles and triumphs, and from the values my Mother instilled in me. I hope that something in these chapters has helped you, and that you'll return to them whenever you need guidance along the way.

> • • • RESOURCE • • •
>
> My website, www.justinskeytohomelife.com, offers ongoing resources, updated content, and ways to continue this conversation beyond what these pages can contain.

CONTINUING THE CONVERSATION

Markets change. Programs evolve. New options emerge. Staying informed helps you adapt and make good decisions as circumstances shift.

The downloadable worksheets mentioned throughout this book are available on my website—financial calculators, maintenance checklists, project planners, and other tools to help you along the way.

If this book has been helpful, I'd be honored if you shared it with others who might benefit. The families I most want to reach—the ones working hard toward homeownership, the ones who need guidance that others won't take time to provide—often find resources through word of mouth rather than advertising.

WHAT MY MOM TAUGHT ME

Everything I've shared in this book connects back to my Mom. The discipline with money. The belief that everyone deserves help, not just the people who already have it figured out. The understanding that home is more than a building—it's where life happens, where families grow, where memories are made.

My Mom never got her dream home. She passed away still imagining that kitchen, that porch, that backyard. Still dreaming about what it would feel like to own something that was truly hers.

For a long time, that broke my heart. I'd spent my whole career helping other families achieve what my own Mother never could. It felt unfair. It felt unfinished.

But somewhere along the way, I started seeing it differently. Her dream didn't die with her. It lives on in every family I help. Every key I hand over carries a piece of what she wanted for us. Every time I watch a mom cry happy tears in her new kitchen, every time I see a family finally get their yes after years of nos—I feel like I'm honoring her memory in the most meaningful way I know how.

She was the best. And the values she taught me—the discipline, the generosity, the belief that everyone deserves a chance—those are what I've tried to pass along in these pages.

YOUR STORY

Now it's your turn. Your story is being written—in the home you find, the memories you create, the stability you build, the legacy you leave.

It won't be perfect. There will be challenges you don't expect, problems that test you, moments when you wonder if it's all worth it. It is. I promise you, it is.

The security of having a place that's truly yours. The pride of ownership. The freedom to make a space reflect who you are. The stability it provides for your family. The wealth you're building. The foundation you're creating for the future. These matter. They're worth the work, the savings, the sacrifices, the challenges along the way.

I believe in you. I believe you can do this.

If you've been told no before, if lenders have turned you away, if you've looked at the numbers and felt like it was impossible—don't give up. I've seen families overcome credit disasters, dig out of debt, save when it seemed like there was nothing left to save, and finally get their keys after years of being told they couldn't. Your past doesn't have to be your future. Start where you are. Do what you can. Keep moving forward.

My Mom believed too. She never stopped believing, even when every door seemed closed, even when the numbers never added up, even when it would have been easier to give up. She held onto that dream until the end.

Hold onto yours. Believe it's possible, even when you can't see exactly how you'll get there. Trust the process. Do the work. Take it one step at a time. And let this book—and me—be part of your journey. Your key to "home" is waiting—go find it.

With sincere gratitude for letting me be part of your journey,

Justin

WWW.JUSTINSKEYTOHOMELIFE.COM

GLOSSARY

• • •

Adjustable-Rate Mortgage (ARM): A mortgage with an interest rate that can change periodically based on market conditions, typically after an initial fixed-rate period.

Amortization: The process of paying off a loan through regular payments that cover both principal and interest over time.

Annual Percentage Rate (APR): The total yearly cost of a loan expressed as a percentage, including interest and certain fees.

Appraisal: A professional assessment of a property's market value, required by lenders before approving a mortgage.

Buyer Agency Agreement: A contract between a home buyer and a real estate agent that establishes the agent's representation of the buyer, including compensation terms. Required following the 2024 National Association of Realtors settlement before touring homes with an agent.

Charge-off: An accounting designation made by a creditor, such as a bank or credit card company, indicating that a debt is unlikely to be collected after a borrower has missed payments for an extended period of time, typically 120 to 180 days.

Closing Costs: Fees and expenses paid at closing to finalize a real estate transaction, typically 2 to 5 percent of the loan amount.

Closing Disclosure: A document detailing final loan terms and closing costs, provided at least three days before closing.

Contingency: A condition in a purchase contract that must be satisfied for the sale to proceed.

Conventional Loan: A mortgage not backed by a government agency, typically requiring higher credit scores and down payments.

Credit Score: A three-digit number (typically 300 to 850) representing creditworthiness based on credit history.

Credit Utilization: The percentage of available credit currently being used, a key factor in credit scores.

Debt-to-Income (DTI) Ratio: The percentage of gross monthly income that goes toward debt payments. Lenders typically require a back-end DTI of 43 percent or less for mortgage approval.

Discount Points: Upfront fees paid to reduce a mortgage interest rate, with each point typically costing 1 percent of the loan amount.

Down Payment: The portion of a home's purchase price paid upfront by the buyer rather than financed.

Earnest Money: A deposit made when submitting an offer, demonstrating good-faith commitment to purchase.

Equity: The difference between a home's market value and the remaining mortgage balance.

Escrow: An account held by a third party to pay property taxes and insurance, or funds held during a transaction.

Federal Housing Administration (FHA) Loan: A mortgage insured by the FHA, with more flexible qualification requirements and down payments as low as 3.5 percent.

Fixed-Rate Mortgage: A mortgage with an interest rate that remains constant for the entire loan term.

Geofencing: Used in many smart thermostats, it is a location-based feature that uses your smartphone's GPS to create a virtual, invisible boundary around your home.

Geothermal Heat Pump: A heating and cooling system that uses the earth's constant underground temperature to provide highly efficient climate control, with significantly longer lifespan than traditional HVAC systems.

Home Equity Line of Credit (HELOC): A revolving credit line secured by your home equity, allowing you to borrow as needed up to a set limit, typically at lower interest rates than credit cards.

Homeowners Association (HOA): An organization that manages a community and enforces rules, funded by mandatory member fees.

Home Equity Loan: A fixed-rate loan that lets you borrow against your home equity in a lump sum, repaid over a set term.

Home Inspection: A professional examination of a property's condition before purchase.

Heating Seasonal Performance Factor (HSPF): A rating that measures the heating efficiency of heat pumps. Higher numbers indicate better efficiency.

Loan Estimate: A document detailing expected loan terms and costs, provided within three days of mortgage application.

Mortgage Insurance: Insurance protecting the lender if a borrower defaults, typically required with down payments below 20 percent.

National Association of Realtors (NAR) Settlement 2024: Industry changes following an NAR legal settlement that restructured how real estate agent commissions are negotiated and disclosed, requiring buyer agency agreements before home tours.

Net Worth: Total assets minus total liabilities; what you own minus what you owe.

Principal, Interest, Taxes, and Insurance (PITI): The main components of a monthly housing payment.

Preapproval: A lender's conditional commitment to make a loan after verifying financial information, including a credit check and documentation review.

Prequalification: A preliminary estimate of borrowing capacity based on unverified information.

Principal: The amount borrowed, excluding interest, or the portion of a payment reducing the loan balance.

Seasonal Energy Efficiency Ratio (SEER): A rating that measures the cooling efficiency of air conditioning systems. Higher numbers indicate better efficiency. Current minimum standards require SEER 14–15, depending on the region.

Smart Thermostat: A programmable thermostat that connects to Wi-Fi and can learn your schedule, be controlled remotely, and optimize heating and cooling for efficiency and comfort.

Title: Legal ownership of property and the right to possess it.

Title Insurance: Insurance protecting against claims on property ownership or undiscovered liens.

Underwriting: The lender's process of evaluating a loan application and assessing risk.

US Department of Agriculture (USDA) Loan: A government-backed mortgage for eligible rural and suburban areas with no down payment required.

Veterans Affairs (VA) Loan: A mortgage guaranteed by the Department of Veterans Affairs for eligible service members and veterans, with no down payment required and no mortgage insurance.

RESOURCES

Download these worksheets free at
www.justinskeytohomelife.com

FINANCIAL FOUNDATION WORKSHEETS

Net Worth Calculator: Track assets and liabilities to understand your starting point.

Monthly Budget Template: Plan and track income and expenses.

Credit Score Action Plan: Identify and address factors affecting your credit.

Debt Elimination Tracker: Organize and track payoff progress using the Momentum Method.

Down Payment Savings Calculator: Determine how much you need and how long it will take.

True Housing Cost Calculator: Budget for all costs of homeownership, not just mortgage payment.

DTI Calculator: Calculate your front-end and back-end DTI ratios to see if you qualify for a mortgage and how much you can afford.

HOME-BUYING WORKSHEETS

Preapproval Document Checklist: Gather all required documents for the mortgage application.

Loan Comparison Worksheet: Compare offers from multiple lenders side by side.

Home Search Priority Matrix: Define and prioritize your needs versus wants.

Property Evaluation Scorecard: Rate and compare properties objectively.

Closing-Cost Estimator: Budget for all closing expenses.

Closing-Day Checklist: Everything you need for a smooth closing.

HOME-IMPROVEMENT WORKSHEETS

Renovation Priority Planner: Identify and sequence improvement projects.

Contractor Comparison Sheet: Evaluate and compare contractor bids.

Project Budget Tracker: Monitor renovation spending against budget.

HOME-MAINTENANCE WORKSHEETS

Seasonal Maintenance Calendar: Schedule and track maintenance tasks throughout the year.

Home Systems Inventory: Record age, warranty, and service details of major systems.

Emergency Contact List: Important numbers for home emergencies.

Download all resources free at
www.justinskeytohomelife.com

Scan to visit the website.

JUSTIN'S KEY TO HOME LIFE

References

• • •

Fannie Mae. *Selling Guide.* Last modified March 4, 2026. https://selling-guide.fanniemae.com/

Freddie Mac. *Seller/Servicer Guide.* Last modified March 4, 2026. https://guide.freddiemac.com

U.S. Department of Housing and Urban Development. *Single Family Housing Policy Handbook 4000.1.* Last modified March 4, 2026. https://www.hud.gov/hud-partners/single-family-handbook-4000-1

U.S. Department of Energy. *Do-It-Yourself Savings Project: Lower Water Heating Temperature.* Last modified March 12, 2025. https://www.energy.gov/energysaver/do-it-yourself-savings-project-lower-water-heating-temperature

U.S. Department of Energy. *LED Lighting.* Last modified March 4, 2026. https://www.energy.gov/energysaver/led-lighting Energy Saver-energy.gov/energysaver/programmable-thermostats

U.S. Department of Energy. *Water Heating.* Last modified March 10, 2025. https://www.energy.gov/energysaver/water-heating

U.S. Energy Information Administration. *Residential Energy Consumption Survey (RECS).* Last modified May 27, 2025. https://www.eia.gov/consumption/residential/

ABOUT THE AUTHOR

• • •

Justin McCurdy has dedicated nearly three decades to the housing industry, building deep expertise spanning new-home construction, resale home sales, mortgage lending, home design, renovations, and smart-home technology. His unique blend of hands-on field experience and financial acumen gives him a perspective few in the industry can match—and he's passionate about sharing it with others.

Justin's expertise in technology and smart-home integration sets him apart in today's rapidly evolving housing market. From automated lighting and climate systems to advanced security and energy-efficient solutions, he helps homeowners understand how modern technology can enhance comfort, safety, and long-term value. His passion for home design and renovation grew naturally from years spent on construction sites, collaborating closely with architects, builders, and tradespeople to bring visions to life.

Justin grew up in poverty in the Midwest, watching his Mom work tirelessly to provide for the family while dreaming of a home she never got to own. That experience shapes everything he does. He's passionate about helping the families that others overlook—the people who need guidance most but often get the least attention.

As a teenager, Justin spent summers framing custom homes alongside experienced crews and working with landscaping companies to shape the exteriors that completed them. Those early years gave him a firsthand understanding of how homes are built from the bones out—from foundation and framing to the curb appeal that makes a house feel like home. That foundation of real, hands-on work informs every piece of advice he offers today.

He has also rebuilt his own credit twice, climbing from low scores to the 800s, and he shares those hard-won lessons throughout this book to help readers do the same.

Justin is actively working in real estate in the United States, with experience spanning three distinct regions of the country. But Justin's Key to Home Life was created for a bigger purpose than any single transaction. It was built to help people everywhere—regardless of where they live or what they earn—achieve the dream of a home life they love and a future they can be proud of.

Through his website, Justin offers resources spanning every aspect of the home experience: home-buying guidance, home-improvement strategies, smart-home technology, interior-design inspiration, and practical financial planning. His goal is to make expert-level knowledge accessible to everyone.

Giving back is at the heart of who Justin is. One of his favorite organizations is the Friends of Finn Foundation (www.friendsoffinn.org), a nonprofit that provides comfort items—blankets, toys, care packages, and emotional support—to children battling cancer and undergoing bone marrow transplants. Justin actively supports the foundation and encourages others to get involved, however they can.

Justin also carries a deeply personal dream of one day creating a foundation in honor of his late Mother to help single mothers achieve homeownership. His Mom spent her life dreaming of a home she never got to own, and while she never walked through that front door, her memory deserves a legacy that opens doors for others. Justin believes that if he can help even one single mother achieve what his own Mother couldn't, her dream will live on.

For Justin, this isn't just a career—it is his life's purpose. If the work he does through this book, his website, and his daily efforts helps people achieve even a fraction of what his Mother spent her life dreaming of, he will consider himself successful.

CONNECT WITH JUSTIN

WWW.JUSTINSKEYTOHOMELIFE.COM

ACKNOWLEDGMENTS

• • •

This book exists because of the hundreds of families who have trusted me to guide them through the home-buying process. Your dreams, your questions, your challenges, your triumphs—they taught me what this book needed to contain. Thank you for letting me be part of your journeys.

To God: Thank You for guiding my path, for carrying me through the darkest times, and for blessing me beyond what I ever deserved. Every good thing in my life flows from You. This book, this career, this family—none of it would exist without Your grace. I'm forever grateful.

To My Mom: You were the best Mother I could have ever hoped for. Everything I am, everything I know about working hard and treating people right, everything I understand about managing money and never giving up—it all started with you. You never got your dream home, but you gave me the values to help others achieve theirs. Every key I hand over honors your memory. I miss you every day. I hope I am making you proud. I love you.

To My Wife: I love you. I'm so lucky to have you by my side. Thank you for all of the support you give me, for loving me as I am, flaws and all. Thank you for being my partner, my best friend, and the heart of our home. Thank you for giving us our beautiful, smart son. I couldn't do any of this without you.

To My Son: I love you more than words can say. I'm so lucky to be your father, and watching you grow into the person you're becoming is the greatest joy of my life. I'm so proud of you already—your curiosity, your kindness, your laughter that fills our home. I can't wait to see the man you become. Always remember that you're worthy of happiness and success. Work hard. Keep your heart open. Believe in yourself, even when it's difficult. Don't be scared to fail—learn from your mistakes and keep moving forward. Always do what you say you'll do. Have honor. Have courage. Give back to others whenever you can. Be brave. Be kind. Know that no matter what, your dad loves you and believes in you completely. You're my greatest blessing.

To My Little Sister: I love you. You shared those years with me and understand where we came from and what our Mom meant to us. We've been through so much together, and I cherish our relationship. Thank you for all of your unwavering support throughout our life together—I'm so lucky to have you as my sister! I'm so proud of the woman you have become. I know Mom is proud of you, too—she's always looking down on you and smiling.

To My Chosen Brothers: I love you. Thank you for sticking by me through the low times and the high times, for accepting me exactly as I am, and for your loyalty that has never wavered. Thank you for the parenting advice, the late-night conversations, the laughter, and the moments when you reminded me who I am when I had forgotten. Every win you achieve makes me feel like I win too. I'm always here for you—no matter what, no matter when. Brotherhood isn't about blood; it's about the people who show up. You've always shown up for me, and I'll always show up for you.

To My Dear Friends: Those in Alabama who helped my family in our darkest hour. You know who you are, and you know what you did for us. When we had nothing, when we didn't know how we would survive, you showed up with open hands and open hearts. You're special beyond words. You impacted my life forever, and I carry what you did for us with me every single day. I pray that God blesses you with the best things in life—you deserve every good thing that comes your way.

To My Big Brother: The one from the Big Brother, Little Brother program, who took a fatherless kid to construction sites and showed him what was possible; who taught me that building homes means building families; and who planted seeds that grew into a career and a calling. Thank you.

To My Colleagues and Mentors: Those who taught me different aspects of this industry over the years. The knowledge in this book isn't mine alone—it is accumulated wisdom from countless professionals who were generous with their expertise.

To Everyone Reading this Book: Thank you for investing in yourself, for refusing to leave something this important to chance, for believing that homeownership is possible for you. May your key unlock not just a door, but a life filled with the stability, joy, and memories that only home can provide.

WWW.JUSTINSKEYTOHOMELIFE.COM

---

www.ingramcontent.com/pod-product-compliance
Lightning Source LLC
LaVergne TN
LVHW011633200926
848484LV00014B/2583/J